Red Dragon Fantasy: Song Lyrics and Poetry

Ryan Keith Johnson

Do not infringe on this publication, plagiarize, reproduce in whole or in part, or store in a retrieval system, or transmit in any form or by any means, electronic, mechanical, photocopy, recording device, illegal downloading, pirating or otherwise, without written permission of the author. For information regarding permission contact email:
funtimewriting_77@yahoo.com , johnsonryan_77@hotmail.com, ryanjohnsoncmps@yahooo.com or contact social networking sites via Facebook or twitter.

All rights reserved by Red and Blue Dragon Fantasy LLC. The author guarantees all contents are original and do not infringe upon the legal rights of any other person or work. All songs, poems via compositions, are written and created by the author, Ryan Keith Johnson. Any illegal tampering, plagiarism any copying and manipulation of any kind will be prosecuted. Up to fines, civil collection for damages or prison or both.

"Red Dragon Fantasy: Song Lyrics and Poetry"
Copy Right © 2019
All rights reserved.
Red and Blue Dragon Fantasy LLC. and Lightning Source.
Cover Design by Ryan Keith Johnson
Photo taken by Dan Grevas
Sales tax included.
ISBN: 978-1-7339815-2-1

Other books:

"The King's Retribution"
"Lion Ascend"
"What I Think About You: Song Lyrics and Poetry"
"The Temple of the Incubus"
"Red and Blue Dragon Fantasy Legacy Anthology
of Compositions and Short Short Stories"
"Blue Dragon Fantasy: Faded Memories and Short Stories"
"The Culminate Amethyst"
"An Angel's Whisper"

Heart Of Hell

Heart Of Hell
Punishment From The Scarecrow
Cobra King
Better Than All Of Them
Loves Disadvantage
Lies And Trickery
Trauma Of Death
Eternity And Infinity
Little Monsters
Arbitrator Of Souls
The Easy One
Black Over Dosage
Fear's Escape

Red Dragon Fantasy; Song Lyrics and Poetry

Heart Of Hell

I can feel the flames burning in my chest
it scorches from my heart, it makes me fall apart
I can sometimes steal the flames from the best
its like lightning and I don't know where to start

its a heart of hell that makes me want to crush the hearts of others
its a deep hatred I feel when I've been done wrong by my sisters and brothers
these sisters and brothers from school that make me feel like a fool
I can feel myself grow stronger as I tell them they're under my foot and I'm not their tool

I'm going to live long
living together with my immediate family and living well
be nice and kind I hear my parents say, but they don't know what I've

Red Dragon Fantasy; Song Lyrics and Poetry

done is there anything you can find in this school to live long and live well? my eyes are open not closed so keep listening

heart of hell	a heart of hell
hard as hell	that keeps me thinking of you
its just as well	as I watch the news of the abuse in
school	
get back in your cell	they go to prison for first degree
murder	

heart of hell	a heart of hell
hard as hell	that keeps people scared of you
its just as well	as I hear rumors of you as the fool
get back for its hot as hell	they're looking for murder

I've been cursed since the day I entered this school
they mock me, they make me a joke, they embarrass me
every day I come to this prison to learn how much I am a fool
I hate everyone, I can't stand to be here, I hate it here and I don't want to see

I feel like I've been cursed since the day I was born
the faculty and the students make me believe they will live long?
I have eyes of doom, my eyes hurt from the pain endured and I'm worn
what is knowledge when it won't help me when I graduate, I don't know what's wrong

I'm going to live long
living together with my immediate family and living well
be nice and kind I hear my parents say, but they don't know what I've done
is there anything you can find in this school to live long and live well? my eyes are open not closed so keep listening

heart of hell	a heart of hell
hard as hell	that keeps me thinking of you

Red Dragon Fantasy; Song Lyrics and Poetry

its just as well	as I watch the news of the abuse in
school	
get back in your cell	they go to prison for first degree
murder	

heart of hell	a heart of hell
hard as hell	that keeps people scared of you
its just as well	as I hear rumors of you as the fool
get back for its hot as hell	they're looking for murder

every day at five in the morning I wake up to get an education.
every day is a life of hell and humiliation can you tell me God
what the fuck kind of life a boy can endure for destructive
communication

its like watching in slow motion of what a boy can do to become a man
pick up a gun from his dad's dresser and load it up
take the bus to school to prove to his bullies that he's more than a man
pull it out from his history book and point it at the bully that teased him
and say
"What's up?" and blow him away

give him a bullet through the brain and then point at yourself before you
pull the trigger
and there my friend is when you have a heart of hell

I'm going to live long
living together with my immediate family and living well
be nice and kind I hear my parents say, but they don't know what I've
done
is there anything you can find in this school to live long and live well?
my eyes are open not closed so keep listening

heart of hell	a heart of hell
hard as hell	that keeps me thinking of you
its just as well	as I watch the news of the abuse in
school	
get back in your cell	they go to prison for first degree

murder

heart of hell	a heart of hell
hard as hell	that keeps people scared of you
its just as well	as I hear rumors of you as the fool
get back for its hot as hell	they're looking for murder

but they're never going to find me!

Punishment From The Scarecrow

I'm the scarecrow
I don't have a brain
my body is filled with straw
I have no confidence I feel so low
I feel like shit and I'm down the drain
I feel like I'm more than a flaw
can someone help me?

I'm the scarecrow
I don't have a brain and I've gone insane
I feel so cold, I feel so empty and raw
I have no reassurance, I lost my soul
I'm at the bottom of this pit and I'm in a lot of pain
I feel guilty, as though I broke the law
can someone help me?

you left me alone
you left me to die
I'm coming after you
don't bother to use the phone
you told me a lie
and there's nothing you can do

punishment from the scarecrow
can you hear me scratching the walls
the crows shall come to pick you apart

Red Dragon Fantasy; Song Lyrics and Poetry

punishment from the scarecrow
can you see me walking towards you
I'm like the devil walking in the dark
punishment from the scarecrow
I'll punch through your chest and rip out your heart
and then I'll rip off your balls

you wake up and realize where you are
you're in a field and nailed to a pole
you see I'm human and you don't know what you are
you realize you're a scarecrow and the crows are on the pole
and you ask me to help you

you are the scarecrow
you don't have a brain
your body is filled with straw
you have no confidence, you feel so low
you feel like shit and you're going down the drain
you feel like you're more than a flaw
can someone help you ?

you left me alone
you left me to die
I'm coming for you
don't bother to use the phone
you told me a lie
and there's nothing you can do

punishment from the scarecrow
can you hear me scratching the walls?
the crows shall come to pick you apart
punishment from the scarecrow
can you see me walking towards you?
I'm like the devil walking in the dark
punishment from the scarecrow
I'll punch through your chest and rip out your heart
and then I'll rip off your balls
punishment from the scarecrow

Cobra King

life in junior high is like a jungle
its hot and humid like a real jungle
every guy is trying to prove to every girl
that he's God's gift of every girl

there's the feeling that I don't care for
this tight competition of what's expected of you
the sexual energy in the air that can be seen outside the door
its like seeing different shades of red and decide which hugh
its like a school of cobras breeding and fighting over the other

raspidy mouth wide open
pending fangs of rage
destructive eyes that plunder
nothing much more than the sound of thunder
hunted down in a cage
watch out for my bite
for you there is nothing better than the night

cobra king
bloody fang
cobra king
bloody fang
eyes of danger

you can see a boy as he does something sweet
its valentine's day and he becomes a man as he gives a girl roses
he becomes a man and the others can see that
they laugh at him, call him names and have him beat
he feels humiliated, sad as he loses
loses the love of his life and feels like a gnat

the girl moves on and feels nothing for him
the snakes have won and look upon their leader to take him
there's no way out and there's no escape from this prison

the eight hours of hell to endure before the last lesson
the last buzzer ring until he can jump on the bus before he's done
just five more years until he's done

raspidy mouth wide open
pending fangs of rage
destructive eyes that plunder
nothing much more than the sound of thunder
hunted down in a cage
watch out for my bite
for you there is nothing better than the night

cobra king
bloody fang
cobra king
bloody fang

cobra king
bloody fang
cobra king
bloody fang
eyes of danger

I can hear the rattles of my body
as I prepare to defend myself
I feel angry as I lash out to destroy everybody

destructive   persuasive   distractive

all these meanings are very possessive

I slither my way out to you
like a rope of death as I try to kill you

raspidy mouth wide open
pending fangs of rage
destructive eyes that plunder
nothing much more than the sound of thunder

hunted down in a cage
watch out for my bite
for you there is nothing better than the night

cobra king
bloody fang   *cobra king*
cobra king
bloody fang   *cobra king*

cobra king
bloody fang   *cobra king*
cobra king
bloody fang   *cobra king*
eyes of danger

Better Than All Of Them

I'm better than all of them
I'm more creative I'm more attractive
I'm better than all of you
I've got stronger family ties and a better attitude
I'm better than all of them
I completed eight novels, twelve books of poetry
I'm better than all of you
I bike fourteen miles a day and sang my music
what can you do?
I'm better than all of you

the memories are twisted with thoughts of my future
a photo of me at sixteen and while I look at my own picture
I drift further away from everyone in sight
my parents can't help me and I can't escape this nightmare at night
I wake up feeling destructive and impassive
as I tell my friends, they become scared while others think impressive
I talk to myself every day and I hope to do better in my future

in my world I became a God
while everyone was busy trying to get a letter grade

Red Dragon Fantasy; Song Lyrics and Poetry

I created my child in seventh grade
I kept him warm and nurtured him until he was whole
I showed him to everyone because he was the love of my life
these memories are twisted like the roots of a dying tree

then he was stolen from me, taken away in plain sight
one-hundred and fifty pages missing with only the cover, I wanted to fight
I felt angry and agony with this institution they call education
only someone so jealous would have wanted to destroy something so great in mind

I'm better than all of them
I'm more creative I'm more attractive
I'm better than all of you
I've got stronger family ties and a better attitude
I'm better than all of them
I completed eight novels, twelve books of poetry
I'm better than all of you
I bike fourteen miles a day and sang my music to the world
what can you do?
I'm better than all of you

I'm better than all of them
I'm more creative I'm more attractive
I'm better than all of you
I've got stronger family ties and a better attitude
I'm better than all of them
I completed eight novels, twelve books of poetry
I'm better than all of you
I bike fourteen miles a day and sang my music to the world
what can you do?
I'm better than all of you

as I look around among a group of low lives, I see a man
who stands over you as he creates eight more and gives them life
they are beautiful and stronger than their older brother that lost his life
twelve of them are babies that will never leave his arms

they will be taught to distrust you all, you want to know who that man is?
that man is me

I think of the way I've been treated
I think of the rank that I've been seated
I've taken enough shit from these sorts of people
that its time to fight back
I hear the rumors spread like disease that I'm gay
I'm so fet up, but I don't know what to say
I hope they get the worse life imaginable, I hope they get stabbed in the back
but now I can't escape this prison with my children until my senior year
I'm just better than all of them and I ain't got nothing to fear

I'm better than all of them
I'm more creative I'm more attractive
I'm better than all of you
I've got stronger family ties and a better attitude
I'm better than all of them
I completed eight novels, twelve books of poetry
I'm better than all of you
I bike fourteen miles a day and sang my music to the world
what can you do?
I'm better than all of you

I'm better than all of them
my parents are better than all of you
I'm better than all of you
my sisters are better than all of you
I'm better than all of them
my grandmas and grandpas are better than you
I'm better than all of you
class mates from outside this town are better than you
I'm better than all of them
I'm better than all of you
so fuck all of you

Red Dragon Fantasy; Song Lyrics and Poetry

Love's Disadvantage

when you're looking at yourself up at ease
and nobody's there   *nobody's there*
you dare to break her heart at once been teased
and its too much to bare

so what's going to happen to you when you make her cry
your hearts still at ease and you feel you are going to die
solitary strikes you so hard and you split up from your love
so when you look to a starlit sky way up above
and see how much love has done for you
what are you willing to do?

so where are you going to cry to now?
when I was still with you and you ran to this time
don't you dare block my internal thoughts about you
for something to love will never die

its love's disadvantage
that you won't go through life without breaking your heart
its love's disadvantage
that the girl won't break her heart for you
its love's disadvantage
that you can't escape getting a heart broken apart
its a love's disadvantage
to fall in love and expect everything to be new
its love's disadvantage
to stand up and be a man for the challenge

so what's going to happen when she makes you cry?
are you going to stand there or go after her ?
solitary strikes you so hard that you feel like you're going to die
so when you look to a starlit sky, way up above
and see how much love has done to you
what is it that it will do you?

when you're looking at yourself up at ease

and nobody's there   *nobody's there*
you dare to break her heart once you've been teased
and its too much to bare

its love's disadvantage
that you won't go through life without breaking your heart
its love's disadvantage
that the girl won't break her heart for you
its love's disadvantage
that you can't escape getting a heart broken apart
its a love's disadvantage
to fall in love and expect everything to be new
its love's disadvantage
to stand up and be a man for the challenge

I can see her sitting in front of me every day in class
I think to myself with a smile about how she is great
a girl in my eyes, but a princess in my dreams with class
I hope when we meet that its fate

its love's disadvantage   *that you can fall in love*
that you won't go through life without breaking your heart
its love's disadvantage   *its greater than what you want*
that the girl won't break her heart for you
its love's disadvantage   *its more than you can handle*
that you can't escape getting a heart broken apart
its a love's disadvantage   *and better than all the rest*
to fall in love and expect everything to be new
its love's disadvantage   *worth more than all the gold in the world*
to stand up and be a man for the challenge
when your hearts at ease and nobody's there
nobody's there nobody's there

Lies And Trickery

out in the woods out in the trees
prepare to do your safe deeds

Red Dragon Fantasy; Song Lyrics and Poetry

you've better escape
you've made your own mistake

run run as fast as you can
damn those who have betrayed you
so run now, don't you come back
you've lost your soul so where will you run?

the people in your village don't care where you've been
they want to know where you are and there's nothing you can do
they want to abuse you, mentally, physically and emotionally to bring you back
you've been sucked dry and your all done so where will you go?

out in the woods, out in the trees
prepare to do your safe deeds
lies and trickery   eyes are prickly
you've better escape
you have made your own mistake
lies and trickery

humanly possible is this true?
do to facts of lies other than truth
so how many deaths will cover the lies
think about it?

throughout history the devs' have sucked people dry
they've spread lies to justify their own truth
people who have loved and honored those who have done wrong
only learn that they were misled and now they know why

out in the woods, out in the trees
prepare to do your safe deeds
lies and trickery   eyes are prickly
you've better escape
you have made your own mistake
lies and trickery

Sunday's coffin waits for you
the devs want you to be an empty shell
before they lie you down and kill you
how much will death get to you?
do you think its worth your life to return and put up a fight?
or will you take it?
a chance to meet death

out in the woods, out in the trees
prepare to do your safe deeds
lies and trickery   eyes are prickly   *eyes are prickly*
you've better escape
you have made your own mistake   *mistake*
lies and trickery

out in the woods, out in the trees
prepare to do your safe deeds
lies and trickery   eyes are prickly   *eyes are prickly*
you've better escape
you've built your own fate   *built your own fate*
lies and trickery
say no more
lies and trickery
lies and trickery

Trauma Of Death

death comes to us all and it waits by the door when we leave
it waits while you drive your car and when you cross the street
it comes to you with a smile and can look like anyone
this thing called death is what I am and I'm looking for you

fast growing beats of your heart is what you can hear
you got into a car accident, senseless and disabled and filled with fear
bleeding blows to your skull like a knife that is dull
embedded in your skull
glass rips through your bones and your soul waits for an answer

Red Dragon Fantasy; Song Lyrics and Poetry

listen to me as I prepare to drag you under
listen to me   listen to me

I've been sent here from the prince of darkness
stricken with lighting, I'm your sudden shock
when your body is locked, you will never move
I am trauma of death

in the grave
less than brave
you could have saved yourself in a hurry by escaping me
if you're alive you will find yourself in a hospital
or wake up in a car wreck
can you hear me call

your body is broken, did you wear your seat belt?
do you think you're still alive or in the afterlife?
you begin to cry from the shock and think about everything you felt
you're single and wish you would have had a wife
but your girlfriend never came to see you in the hospital

listen to me as I prepare to drag you under
listen to me   listen to me

I've been sent here from the prince of darkness
stricken with lighting I'm your sudden shock
when your body is locked you will never move
I am trauma of death

thrown around like a bat out of hell
once deceased you will join me now
you will know that you have no nine lives
strapped into the surgery room
not even they can save you because after anesthesia then comes me
fate of doom comes across to you

listen to me as I prepare to drag you under
listen to me   listen to me

I've been sent here from the prince of darkness
stricken with lighting I'm your sudden shock
when your body is locked you will never move
I am trauma of death

listen to me as I prepare to drag you under
listen to me   listen to me

I've been sent here from the prince of darkness
stricken with lighting I'm your sudden shock
when your body is locked you will never move
I am trauma of death

Infinity And Eternity

anything and everything that you never thought could exist, exists
space and time are unified in infinity
like the number eight that symbolizes eternity
nobody knows what's there that exists
beyond imagination and languages, could be light years from here

predicting the future with the power of the stars
nobody knows how or why it happens, but they know when it happens
no way to continue in this burning hell, full of wars
let's take a rocket and shoot it through space and see what happens

all that we've seen everywhere this place
infinity eternity
infinity eternity
infinity eternity

in the future far past our lives
we will search for life no matter where it lies
flying through the empty space we witness the birth of a star
we turn to the left and then to the right and see how it dies
we fight hard, we fight long and we pay for it with our lives

all that we've seen everywhere this place
infinity eternity
infinity eternity
infinity eternity

on what was to have begun
on what was to have happened
witness the end of the star
or the birth of the sun
watch as we witness something new happen
infinity eternity

all that we've seen
infinity eternity
infinity eternity
infinity eternity

The Little Monsters

they harvest under your bed
soft goodnight prayers will not do as said
do not speak   do not talk
for in fear they will turn to your door
sleep and wake up suddenly with tears of fear
they live to play jokes on your mind and who knows when they will come
flared into sleeplessness, wake up to see what it could be now

you should be scared of them
just like everyone else should be scared of them
half past midnight and you can hear something open the door
hiding under the covers won't make them leave your bed
you have to witness what you hear
because they want you dead
they want to kill you and they will make your body numb

shrouding back and forth

turning side to side
wakening in horror you see them coming
coming for you in dreams of horror
sudden crashing from your mind of dreams in the night

creeping beside your bed side in hope of scare
truth to truth
lies to lies
for the little monsters its all a game that is fair
ganging up against you is what it is and what will you do?
cuts and bruises which should be nothing new to you
you wake up in horror from seeing the little monsters
shouting in laughter   start running faster

you're trapped in your room
and there's no way to escape
the little monsters are here and give you doom
they're ready to cut you into pieces, a never ending rape
after they've polished your bones they'll wear your bones like its fate

they're carrying their little spears and knock down the door
they're engraved to you fear as they jump on your bed
you howl in your self-pity and pain of the horror
how will you escape? as you stare at the broken door
the door is broken and you wonder what will happen when you're dead
you think you've encountered fate, but you wake up with your parents shaking you up

shrouding back and forth you see it was just a dream
turning side to side you realize nothing is what it seems
you woke up the dead with your deadly scream
you thought they were coming for you in dreams of horror
but you realize it was all a dream but look at the broken door
and wonder if it was real

shrouding back and forth
turning side to side
wakening in horror you see them coming

coming for you in dreams of horror
sudden crashing from your mind of dreams in the night

creeping beside your bed side in hope of scare
truth to truth
lies to lies
for the little monsters its all a game that is fair
ganging up against you is what it is and what will you do?
cuts and bruises which should be nothing new to you
you wake up in horror from seeing the little monsters
shouting in laughter   start running faster

Arbitrator Of Souls

I know the power I have when I'm angry, its like death
and I feel like stealing other people's breath
its foreseen to you and there's nothing you can do

sometimes I feel like I'm fate
stealing other people's sanity
stealing others new wisdom
and stealing their energy
for my own personal gain

distraction
destruction
I will take your sudden reaction

arbitrator of souls
ruler of destruction
arbitrator of souls

when I feel angry, I get destructive with my pride
all of the ones I've hurt have cried
for the pain and suffering brought upon me I only wish death for them
for the destruction of my child I would like their soul
I would like to rip their body apart, I'll make them howl
try getting revenge with me I would like to see

your friends are ruled under me

distraction
destruction
I will take your sudden reaction

arbitrator of souls
ruler of destruction
arbitrator of souls

my mind is full and my nails are sharp
taking my time, waiting for the perfect time
to decide the perfect crime
the decision is mine
look into my eyes that are red
you dare mock me to my face
you'll learn by what was said
supernatural dread

distraction
destruction
I will take your sudden reaction

arbitrator of souls
ruler of destruction
arbitrator of souls

arbitrator of souls
ruler of destruction
arbitrator of souls
arbitrator of souls
arbitrator of souls

The Easy One

toll ho
to the city of corruption

Red Dragon Fantasy; Song Lyrics and Poetry

your faced in my destruction
you know you better stay on the other side
the others of your kind have lacked this provision
so don't' listen to other people just make up your own decision
so now of this solution so come up with your own conclusion

here in this world I was an eight year old child going to school so that I could be
here in this world I was learning and using my imagination so I can see
then you struck me down, plain as a child and told me I could never be free
instead of being myself you told me I have to be like everyone else I see
but everyone else doesn't have to attend your class and they can be
they don't have to be the easy one

the easy one
so make the sacrifice   *and kill yourself trying*
down is down
sacrifice   *and kill yourself lying*
the easy one

I'm the easy one
an easy choice for the teachers of my choice to make money off of me
I'm the easy one
the one who pays the price and must be different than my class mates
I'm the easy one
the one who can be abused, emotionally, mentally and physically
I'm the easy one

welcome people
to the city of corruption and destruction
death to you will come in a decent function
sacrifice
death to the human race
I'm fet up with this case
up to your face in case you haven't heard
shoot up shoot high as high as the fucking birds
shut off the lights   shut off the lights

the easy one
so make the sacrifice   *and kill yourself trying*
down is down
sacrifice   *and kill yourself lying*
the easy one

shut off the light
never end the fight
tell the people I hate to go to hell
the end of the world, hell who knows who will tell
end of you shall be
do as much as you can do
to fuck up this world that I lie in as it already is

I look around as a child and see
I don't deserve to be in this class
and have a teacher call government officials on me
have a teacher grab my neck because I don't care for her class
fuck you I say, you should be fired and sit in prison

the easy one
so make the sacrifice   *and kill yourself trying*
down is down
sacrifice   *and kill yourself lying*
the easy one

I'm the easy one   *the easy one*
an easy choice for the teachers of my choice to make money off of me
I'm the easy one   *the easy one*
the one who pays the price and must be different than my class mates
I'm the easy one   *the easy one*
the one who can be abused, emotionally, mentally and physically
I'm the easy one   *the easy one*

tolly ho
to this city of corruption
your faced in my destruction

you know you better stay on the other side
the others of your kind have lacked this provision
so don't listen to other people just make up your own decision
so now with this solution come up with your own conclusion

Black Over Dosage

scratch out of softness
blended with darkness
oh what a scary place
now I am in darkness
away from sharpness
oh what a scary place

I am in darkness and I can't find my way out
its a cruel world that I live in and there's no way out
they like to laugh, humiliate me and it feels like I'm being stabbed by knives
I over dosed on sleeping pills, but they can't stop the pain or escape
right now I'm stuck in a world of darkness wishing I was still alive
and God is this a scary place

oh God you're the love of my life
this scary
oh please won't you help me my love
this is scary
oh God won't you come and run
to help me

now I am lost oh what is the cost
wont you come and help me?
swallowed in darkness unfolded in blindness
won't you help me?

while I'm under I can see my sister in the same boat as me
the kids in her class are cruel to her, much more than I can see
I go and comfort her, I tell her it will be ok
but she says it won't be and I can tell she doesn't want to be alive

they make fun of her because she's my sister
they beat her up and make her believe she shouldn't be alive
she shakes her head and says she's not ok
I can see her over dosing on pills and escape from her life
and I think to myself this is scary

oh God you're the love of my life
this scary
oh please won't you help me my love
this is scary
oh God won't you come and run
to help me

I bury my nails
would you put me in jail
they're waiting for me to fail
how can I be lost when I am ok
but I'll never see the light of day
                      never see the light of the day

they make fun of us for uniting
me and my sister and spread rumors about our strength
nobody understands how powerful we are together
they only fear what they don't understand and that we are strength
and as we stand together against the world we can leave forever
from this scary world

I can see my life is getting thin
for now I have paid for my sin
this is scary
but I can see I'm pulling through
I'll open my eyes and come with you

oh God you're the love of my life
this scary
oh please won't you help me my love
this is scary
oh God won't you come and run

to help me
oh won't you please, won't you save me?

oh God you're the love of my life
this is scary
this is scary

Fear's Escape

waking up in a full nights sweat
grappling for tomorrows lesson
tolerance's aggression

I'm so afraid of what will happen to me tomorrow
I don't need an education because of what I have to endure
I'm so angry of what will happen to me tomorrow
I wish I could be home schooled, the simple cure
it's fear's escape, a new lesson, a hopeful cure

fear's escape
fear's escape
fear's escape
give me emotion

I'm trembling from the thunder
when I look at other people and see them as a mirror
from their body, but I see that they're dead inside and it makes me wonder
they stumble and find themselves on the edge where they think its a cure
these people are my class mates and they are like moths flying to light post
they feel satisfied, but little do they know that they are going to roast
its fear's escape, a new lesson, a hopeful cure

fear's escape
fear's escape
fear's escape

give me emotion

hidden cries for sudden good-byes
you can feel your soul was severed in size
come with me
join me now
expel the fear inside *the simple cure*

fear's escape
fear's escape
fear's escape
give me emotion

Join Or Die

The Little Python
Join Or Die
The Runaway
Nightmare Catcher
Alone
Outer Shell
Black Over Dosage II
Broken Away
The Thirteenth Pin
My Die
Perfect Soldier
Old Iron Sides
Undomestic Animals

The Little Python

I can hear the sound of tearing and I can see a rip
there is a slice to my knees
blood is spilling all over the floor
you reach your fingers to the ceiling for help and you're silenced by the seize
you can feel something grab you and pull you along the bloody floor

you fight this monster that's had satisfaction to hunt for kill
you're scared because you're unknown to the skill
you begin to relax and feel a new sensation to become the monster
for soon you will be a monster and you will have your own prey

convenient, eminent, let the tricks be free

shifting on, from passage to passage
shot from hell you're caught in a cage
turned off course to the evil little python
you become just like your enemy, the little python
slithering on, from tunnel to drain
out from hell you're caught in the rain
turned off course and nothing is the same, for the little python
you become just like your enemy, the little python

you clamped down your next victim
and have their limbs spread out with nails driven down
you feel like you're doing justice by torturing your victim
you have a creative little mind, but your face is disfigured
your victim is cut from proportion and you hear him scream
it feels good, it feels fulfilling after you've fell down
like a snake that prefers its prey fresh you go after what you've endured
after your last bite and wash the bones you're re-deemed

convenient, eminent, let the tricks be free

shifting on, from passage to passage

shot from hell you're caught in a cage
turned off course to the evil little python
you become just like your enemy, the little python
slithering on, from tunnel to drain
out from hell you're caught in the rain
turned off course and nothing is the same, for the little python
you become just like your enemy, the little python

you feel discouragement from the perception
you learn that you're really screwed up with no intention
you're a loser with thoughts to torture and enjoy every condition

you're not even human you can feel your reptilian skin
you've been eating other people's skin and mischievous you have been
you're no longer human so prepare to pay for your sin

convenient, eminent, let the tricks be free

shifting on, from passage to passage
shot from hell you're caught in a cage
turned off course to the evil little python
you become just like your enemy, the little python
slithering on, from tunnel to drain
out from hell you're caught in the rain
turned off course and nothing is the same, for the little python
you become just like your enemy, the little python

let the tricks be free!

Join Or Die

come with me to fix our dreams
just to help us and give us a chance
broken chains and revealed beams
just hear me well and give me a chance, oh grace

take your last sip and end the taste
everything has hit me so hard in the face

everything has hit me so hard in the face
oh please don't let me die all as known

its everything we need to learn, at last
its everything we can learn in Barlow's class
the coming together of the USA
the thirteen broken python comes together
nothing can stop the beginning of a nation what else can I say
we'll stand for freedom together, forever

you better join or die
I can hear the redcoats are marching through
join or die
we're here to seek the truth
join or die
ignite yourself for freedom
join or die
prepare to fight for your freedom
join or die

battle after battle the measure of a man and the new nation is tested
swept into darkness when a man falls and only the stars on the flag are crested
come with me as I look around and see that I was here
I'm hiding down below and see a red coat walking near
I hold my breath and try not to scream in terror

its everything we need to learn, at last
its everything we can learn in Barlow's class
the coming together of the USA
the thirteen broken python comes together
nothing can stop the beginning of a nation what else can I say
we'll stand for freedom together, forever

you better join or die
I can hear the redcoats are marching through
join or die
we're here to seek the truth

join or die
ignite yourself for freedom
join or die
prepare to fight for your freedom
join or die

we gather around with sticks and stones
oh we're here for our own and to start a nation
we feel we're alone with fear for England taking our freedom
from now on we'll take our stand, our ground, and fight with passion

my ears are ringing, my heart is beating faster
a redcoat has taken his shot, blew off my leg
knocking me down, bringing me down
making me think, thinking about my memories and freedom
I may die today, but my nation will live together forever

its everything we need to learn, at last
its everything we can learn in Barlow's class
the coming together of the USA
the thirteen broken python comes together
nothing can stop the beginning of a nation what else can I say
we'll stand for freedom together, forever

you better join or die   *join or die*
I can hear the redcoats are marching through
join or die   *join or die*
we're here to seek the truth
join or die   *join or die*
ignite yourself for freedom
join or die   *join or die*
prepare to fight for your freedom
join or die   *join or die*
the coming together of the USA the *USA*

The Runaway

could have been gone , could have been done

out in the sun, nowhere else to run
out in the streets, in the middle of no where

uncharted places   dis-trustful faces
undying crises   everybody lies
survival lessens   its a new lesson
dis-trustful mind   go see what you can find

all that I've been traveling for
I hope to survive and my body feels sore
looking forward vision to the door
outside vision to that I will see
loose foot to my knee, outside it is I will be

could have been lost
in a different town or city
I may have been known
in another county or state, away from pity
serenity is a place to go on , where you won't be worn
I don't have enough money please don't tell me the cost

all that I've been traveling for   *and I'll keep running away from you*
I hope to survive and my body feels sore   *feeling sad and you won't know what to do*
looking forward vision to the door   *I know that they won't catch up to me*
outside vision to that I will see   *I know these roads better than you*
loose foot to my knee, outside it is I will be   *I'll be gone for good, nothing you can do*
for I am the runaway

everything that I've been running away from   *the runaway is in my mind*
I hope to survive and my body feels its time has come   *everything is undone*
I'm looking forward to running for the door   *tell me what*

you find
I can see outside and feel the burning in my core   *the burning in*
my heart
loose foot to my knee, outside I will be to the sun   *I feel like I won*
for I am the runaway   *when*
can I start?
for I am the runaway

Nightmare Catcher

in the night you will be in fate
in a fight you're not going to survive this hate

you could have a nightmare a sudden heart attack in the night
I could be your nightmare when you want to get into a fight
you could have nightmare of me strangling you really tight
I could be your nightmare taking away your sight
a nightmare catcher is what I am
a nightmare catcher is what I am

I'm going to go and see how everything is done to you
through you're facial expression of fear who'd knew
I'm seeing in your eyes the massive venture to your mind
your memories are locked and all is blocked, there's nothing to find

in the night you will be in fate
in a fight you're not going to survive this hate

gone
gone to the end you will know to what it is
done
done out of sin you're to know of the risk

go!

you could have a nightmare, a sudden heart attack in the night
I could be your nightmare when you want to get into a fight
you could have nightmare of me strangling you really tight

I could be your nightmare taking away your sight
a nightmare catcher is what I am
a nightmare catcher is what I am

so why don't you just take off
and you'll find how far you are
there out to get you, there at your door step

I'm going to go and see how everything has been done to you
through you're facial expression of fear who'd knew
I'm seeing in your eyes the massive venture to your mind
your memories are locked and all is blocked, there's nothing to find

in the night you will be in fate
in a fight you're not going to survive this hate

gone to the end you will know what it is
done out of sin you are to know of the risk

oh shit

you could have a nightmare a sudden heart attack in the night
I could be your nightmare when you want to get into a fight
you could have nightmare of me strangling you really tight
I could be your nightmare taking away your sight
a nightmare catcher is what I am
a nightmare catcher is what I am

in the night they will grasp for you
and there is nothing in the night that they would do to you
helpless hand, gone off hand in my hand
you've been lost from them

so in the night you will be in fate
in a fight you're not going to survive this hate

you could have a nightmare a sudden heart attack in the night
I could be your nightmare when you want to get into a fight

you could have nightmare of me strangling you really tight
I could be your nightmare taking away your sight
a nightmare catcher is what I am
a nightmare catcher is what I am

in the night you will be in fate
in a fight you're not going to survive this hate

Alone

you can declare war upon yourself
you can come down with the disease of fear
there is nothing left to fight and you don't have your health
over tight from someone else with wealth
if these are words that you want to hear
than I don't want to be around you

you can be with all your scummy friends
I would rather be alone than to commit sin
I can be my own best friend and not worry about you
these words I say may frighten you
I can get used to being alone and there's nothing you can do

alone   in a whole different world
alone   keeping to myself this time
alone   I enjoy being by myself this time

alone   in a world of being one
alone   sit in my home and drink some wine
alone   in my home that I call my world

no one is here
no one is near
and I'm glad
gone and split away from insanity
I escaped from the mental breakdown
I escaped the people that gave me insanity
we really are alone

alone in this place
no one is here
no one is near and I'm glad
they can't justify what is fantasy and what is reality

alone   in a whole different world
alone   keeping to myself this time
alone   I enjoy being by myself this time

alone   in a world of being one
alone   sit in my home and drink some wine
alone   in my home that I call my world

others say this solitude is impossible
how can this be, how can this be done?
done to the point of being alone
I'm gone to the end to be gone that they brought unto me
devil's hammer has struck unto me

alone   in a whole different world
alone   keeping to myself this time
alone   I enjoy being by myself this time

alone   in a world of being one
alone   sit in my home and drink some wine
alone   in my home that I call my world

Outer Shell

deserted to the end
crystallized and then crushed into nothing
how could this be? where we will not enter
a cross section figure in the distance, you dig deep to the center
a screwed up intention, out of step and out of date
for soon this will be considered fate

can you cut through a rock to get to me?
can you cut through a tree to touch me ?

can you break through ice to grab me?
can you break through my outer shell and kill me?

outer shell   just try to get through my hold
outer shell   come on yield before me
outer shell   just try to get through my hold
you can't get to me

buried up intention and give me a fracture
build up some heat to melt away the cold
for soon this innocence will be twice as pure
cleared up the mind simply done to make you cut off your hold
gone because of time and you don't have a cure
screwed up intuition you suddenly see the whole picture

outer shell   just try to get through my hold
outer shell   come on yield before me
outer shell   just try to get through my hold
you can't get to me

oh gracious me oh what have they done to me
they have done to have broken free
oh prison me just as much as killed me
just let them be

outer shell   just try to get through my hold
outer shell   come on yield before me
outer shell   just try to get through my hold
you can't get to me

outer shell   just try to get through my hold
outer shell   come on yield before me
outer shell   just try to get through my hold
you can't get to me

Black Over Dosage II

I never knew what life meant to me

life as mine was so beautiful to see
I thought it could last forever
the love for you would never be
for now I remember how it should be

I'm sitting in my bath tub with my wrists cut
blood is mixing with the water and I stick my head under
I can't remember much and my mind wanders away
I'm somewhere dark with the spot light on me
its judgment that asks me why?

oh God you're the love of my life
this is scary
oh God you're the love of my life
this is scary
oh God you're the love of my life
this is scary

I never knew how cold death could be
but now with death I finally can see
how life wasn't so bad and I want to go back
I realize how much you mean to me
for now I have learned from my sins now I can see
my life has awakened, and let me open my eyes
let me take my breath

oh God you're the love of my life
this is scary   this is scary
oh God you're the love of my life
this is scary   this is scary
oh God you're the love of my life
this is scary   this is scary

how can I be lost when I am ok
to never see the light of day
my face rises from this tub of blood
renewed for life now hear what I say
I am here to stay

oh God you're the love of my life
this is scary   this is scary
oh God you're the love of my life
this is scary   this is scary
oh God you're the love of my life
this is scary   this is scary

Broken Away

mass mass depression gone to mass dehydration
bits and bits of confrontation destroy this if you will

you can take mortal human beings and smash them like glass
like a new nation that is clean, you can corrupt it with the wrong people
you can take a man and woman and destroy them at last
make them smile make them happy they'll think its wonderful
and make them feel they can't break away

I'm under consideration not to take any more
I will not be broken like glass
but just wait to consider fate hard as to the core
schools, courts and police force will select their cast
but they'll never stop me from breaking away

broken away
broken away
broken away
I cannot stand this any longer
I will not stand for this any more
broken away
broken away

mass mass destruction gone to mass mass manipulation
bits and bits of counterfeit with destruction
just try to get rid of this if you will
you can take children from school and smash them like glass
like a new school that is clean, you can destroy it with the wrong people

make the child smile, brainwash them to think its wonderful
and make them feel they can't break away
then they won't break away

I'm under consideration not to take any more
I will not be broken like glass
but just wait to consider fate hard as to the core
schools, courts and police force will select their cast
but they'll never stop me from breaking away

broken away
broken away
broken away
I can not stand this any longer
I will not stand for this any more
broken away
broken away

| tomorrow news | things I choose | I myself shall try |
| pondering lies | wondering eyes | I myself shall die |

broken dreams shattered dreams open beams
I am broken, I am falling, into an endless pit
send me away from here to a place that resembles prison,   a school
so I can be brainwashed to fit into society again

broken away
broken away
broken away
I cannot stand this any longer
I will not stand for this any more
broken away
broken away

The Thirteenth Pin

you've gone insane, all for within your pride

you feel the pain in your chest and all that you have to find
don't you dare think of this as a disruption
in case for what you have lost and what you've gained
you fake your life for a massive revolution
a massive fight will become your massive resolution

take a hold of your life of what you want
take a grip of your achievement and go for what you really want
don't let anyone tell you what to do
if they say no you can't do that
take a stand for what you believe in and do just that

its all in the pin
feel the cries of your sudden rage
hear the cries of the others in need
its all in the pin
they'll be feeling really bloody
they'll be hoping that they're bloody
its all in the pin

there are so many different ways
to kill the ones that stand in the way
choose which one you want
choose the right one you want
defy any cheap alliance with traitors for tomorrow's death
look once more to the eyes of those near as you take your last breath
take a stand for what you believe in and do just that

its all in the pin
feel the cries of your sudden rage
hear the cries of the others in need
its all in the pin
they'll be feeling really bloody
they'll be hoping that they're bloody
its all in the pin

reused or lost, they can be condemned
destructive they have accused others for witchcraft

they are useless in society for what they have demeaned
they will be screaming to the injection of pain from the sharp needles
given to the hands of the devil's darkness
jealousy isn't honesty and lying the world isn't the truth
a woman lies to her husband as she has sex with her neighbor
there's honesty's proof

hear a woman screaming
hear a man shouting
hear the children crying
hear the public laughing

see a woman screaming
see a man shouting
see the children crying
watch the public laughing

take a stand for what you believe in and do just that

its all in the pin
feel the cries of your sudden rage
hear the cries of the others in need
its all in the pin
they'll be feeling really bloody
they'll be hoping that they're bloody
its all in the pin

its all in the pin
feel the cries of your sudden rage
hear the cries of the others in need
its all in the pin
they'll be feeling really bloody
they'll be hoping that they're bloody
its all in the pin

after the twelfth pin comes the worst death
after death they become nothing because there is nothing

My Die

I longed for life, a happy life, to be one of the cool kids at school
I've typed all I can to experience what it is like to be so cool
I've been damaged and my patience has worn thin from damaged love
they smile and blow me away from here and now I feel unloved

the cool kids at school think I'm different because of my religion
I'm not a clone, I am myself and don't understand my own religion
I'm not invited to their birthday parties
I'm not allowed to play ball with some of them
I'm not able to come to the Christmas parties
the other parents and teachers say I don't belong with them
it brings tears to my eyes when I can't make new friends
because of a religion

I feel like I'm going nowhere and nobody wants me
my sister is going nowhere for the cool girls don't want her either
I can see her crying on the phone begging a cool girl to talk to her
but not me because I feel like I'm dead and becoming less of the old me

its my die
living off of agony
my die
I feel like jumping off to take my own life
its my die
I'm in my own solitude
its my die
a big escape from a world of pain
its my die

everyone makes mistakes even for the cool kids at my school
when I make a mistake, they laugh and make fun of me for weeks
I don't understand where I went wrong to be labeled a fool
they like to laugh, they like to point and gossip about my family for weeks
its a time for birthdays, a time for Christmas and nobody invites me
and nobody wants me

my sister wanted to be part of the cool girls, but she never succeeds
they laugh and point and tell her how dumb she is, which makes her bleed
nobody in this whole world will ever know how strong we were as brother and sister
none of the cool kids in my school know what its like when you contemplate death
living every day in emotional abuse and finding out the cool girls beat up my sister
I could see myself taking my life and I could see my sister take her last breath

its my die
living off of agony
my die
I feel like jumping off to take my own life
its my die
I'm in my own solitude
its my die
a big escape from a world of pain
its my die

I can hear the cool kids talk about my mistakes and it cuts my skin
they think its funny and chipping away at my ego until it wears thin
they'll start laughing and make me and my family a comical joke
if I have to put up with this for six years before I graduate
I think I'll be dead or become somebody in life who is a big joke
I don't want to endure it any longer, but I feel it perpetuate
I don't want to be part of the cool kids at my school
because I would rather be dead

its my die
living off of agony
my die
I feel like jumping off to take my own life
its my die

its my die
I've lost my innocence
its my die
and I'll take my own life
its my die

I'm in my own solitude   *away from people who lie*
its my die   *its my die*
a big escape from a world of pain   *and I'll never be the same*
its my die   *its my die*

The Perfect Soldier

do you remember the Trojan war?
it wasn't a forgotten war
the American flag shall still stand alone
it seems like every year we prepare for another war
prepare for another war and load up your gun
line up, straighten up, chase the enemy on the run

you can be a soldier and do as your told
you can be a man and serve your country
you can listen to the president and decimate a nation
shoot your enemy to pieces, let the war unfold
let loose the bombers, let in the infantry
no time to wait, no time to use your imagination

no time for thrilling fears
no time for chilling tears
in time, this time, laws you will obey
and become
become, the perfect soldier
become, the unstoppable machine

slave
you are a slave
you shall guard my domain
everyone around you dies, but you remain
no one lurks near, no one knows what to hear
a politician's law and everyone lives in fear
master
I am your master, the politician slave master
I am the key to your freedom

you will do what I say
when I say

no time for thrilling fears
no time for chilling tears
in time, this time, laws you will obey
and become
become, the perfect soldier
become the unstoppable machine

trained for the war
no mistakes are present
for you
go on open to the door
for the chance of freedom
young lives of men will be taken

do you remember the Trojan war?
it wasn't a forgotten war
the American flag shall still stand alone
it seems like every year we prepare for another war
prepare for another war and load up your gun
line up straighten up chase the enemy on the run

no time for thrilling fears
no time for chilling tears
in time, this time, laws you will obey
and become
become, the perfect soldier
become the unstoppable machine

you can become the perfect soldier
become the perfect soldier
become the unstoppable machine
you're the perfect soldier
you're the unstoppable machine
no one can stop you

Old Iron Sides

its a war that will get the rebellion crushed
they're unaware of it and it will bust their face
they're inches buried under ash in the cities and everyone is off pace
they're gone   they're done
they're the master race

old time famous British move
old crises   fetish doom
no more escaping moves, no more fiendish move
you are trapped under their sight

the old plans have worked on us
they're on either side
crushing us by the old iron sides
you could have been crushed by now
you have better get done by now
so you will escape or be in next week's fate

downward shattered guns, no more prejudice shall be done
do you think you have left by now? For you will have won
leave your wives behind and fight a war that is already here
leave the love that brought you here and make a stand against your fear
thirteen strips and thirteen star s will rise in the air against the British to prove we won

old time famous British move
old crises   fetish doom
no more escaping moves no more fiendish move
you are trapped under their sight

the old plans have worked on us
they are on either side
crushing us by the old iron sides
you could have been crushed by now
you have better get done by now
so you will escape or be in next week's fate

I can feel the iron hand twisting my throat
cutting off my air supply and I'm losing all hope
I can feel my resurrection to one's own mind
I'll look for you and there you wait to find
a man who died for freedom

slide down state by state
the sudden slap
crashing of the old iron sides
no way to escape the fiendish evil rides
the iron sides   the gate to war

the old plans have worked on us
they're on either side
crushing us by the old iron sides
you could have been crushed by now
you have better get done by now
so you will escape or be in next week's fate

Undomestic Animals

do you hear the whispers in the crowded jungle?
can you see all the animals in a hidden jumble
can you see the animals run in a huge rumble?

cross the rivers   if you dare
crossing the river   it is rare
think   you may think its unfair
but its completely normal to live in the wild
its like watching the behavior of a young child
and no one will care

they're undomestic animals
things they say, are they really criminal?
things they play   are undomestical
are they undomestic animals?

they have scary eyes and sometimes it can be a bad surprise
                          and sometimes it can be a rumor of lies
you're a lot deeper than you realize
                          and it will leave you paralyzed
this ain't no time to play a game
                          and you'll realize you'll never be the same
do you hear the whispers in the crowded jungle?
can you see all the animals in a hidden jumble?
can you see the animals run in a huge rumble?

we have undomestic pride to live in the jungle
we have hidden while some of us have died
you know its your turn to live in the jungle
you will know who preys on you and you must hide
your animal senses shed light to a world in crises
and if you live long enough you'll become one of the wisest

cross the rivers   if you dare
crossing the river   it is rare
think   you may think its unfair

but its completely normal to live in the wild
its like watching the behavior of a young child
and no one will care

they're undomestic animals *undomestic animals*
things they say, are they really criminal? *are they really criminals?*
things they play   are undomestical *are undomestical*
are they undomestic animals? *undomestical animals*
they're undomestic animals *undomestic animals*
things they say, are they really criminal? *are they really criminals?*
things they play   are undomestical *are undomestical*
are they undomestic animals? *undomestical animals*

do you hear the howls and cries?
where you look directly up to the sky
and figure it is thyself who is the hunter

they're undomestic animals *undomestic animals*
things they say, are they really criminal? *are they really criminals?*
things they play   are undomestical *are undomestical*
are they undomestic animals? *undomestical animals*
they're undomestic animals *undomestic animals*
things they say, are they really criminal? *are they really criminals?*
things they play   are undomestical *are undomestical*
are they undomestic animals? *undomestical animals*

Private Devastation

The Wake
Said And Done
Silent Room
Devastation
Immortality
Agitation
Warm Envy
Private
Bring It On
Morale
Doomsday Paper Mesh-a
Heart of Hell II

The Wake

buried in the ground and left to be senseless
cared for as a child and left be defenseless
put away, far away
to be persecuted by these teachers
gone insane and I'm only nine years old
I've gone insane to the end
nothing you can mend
we'll have to see what will unfold

lie down	into the deep
ends	of the earth
sins	in hope of rebirth
death	to me so it can be

I feel like I'm lying in a casket at a wake
everyone that knows me walks past to see
what I once was and what I am now, as an empty shell
for what these teachers have done to me
come and visit me at the wake

this teacher likes to play games
she likes to keep me within parameters
keep me within my own mind
so she can keep her job and feel important
I hope for dread for this child molesting bitch
that others can find that there is a sign
that this she devil is poisoning my mind
she helps the society
by destroying the society
strike me down
tie me down
tenacious me
we shall see

lie down	into the deep
ends	of the earth

sins	in hope of rebirth
death	to me so it can be

I feel like I'm lying in a casket at a wake
everyone that knows me walks past to see
what I once was and what I am now, as an empty shell
for what these teachers have done to me
come and visit me at the wake

I'm buried in the ground and left to be restless
I was cared for as a child and left with destructiveness
put away similar to a prison, in a prison, and there's no effectiveness
to be persecuted by these teachers who want me to be powerless
now they think I'm insane and I'm only nine years old
I think I've gone insane to the end
and there's nothing I can do to win
we'll have to wait a while and then we'll see who's powerless

lie down	into the deep
ends	of the earth
sins	in hope of rebirth
death	to me so it can be

I feel like I'm lying in a casket at a wake
everyone that knows me walks past to see
what I once was and what I am now, as an empty shell
for what these teachers have done to me
come and visit me at the wake

Said And Done

don't argue with me, I'm tired of what you put unto me
don't do, don't think, don't say
don't you think of what you should delay?
because I don't like you   of what you are
and I'm feeling my adrenaline rush to destroy the person I see

I saw you throw the spit wad in my face

you think you're great, but you're not a fair jock
you think you're funny, but you're nothing but a disgrace
I may not be smart, but your about as intelligent as a rock
I can see your look as I get up from my desk and start pounding your face

its said and done
don't' you ever run
come here as done
its said and done
don't you ever run
come here as done
because its said and done

don't be saying things when you can't back it up
you will never see me the same, that way again
don't you act on things without realizing that its a sin
we could have been friends from another life
you could have avoided my burst of destruction from within
a writer getting into fight with a jock in Barlow's class, give it up
two men sharing a great name and yet nobody will win
two little kings fighting over something that left the other in pain
and you know how rumors spread in school
like a poison that spreads through a rose and takes its life
now you know what it's like to feel like a fool

    love   like you hated it   like you hated me

its said and done
don't' you ever run
come here as done
its said and done
don't you ever run
come here as done
because its said and done

hear me   you can hear me screaming
hell to see   you can hear me shouting

see me   walking towards you
do to me   swinging my arms, with my fists in your face

its said and done
don't' you ever run
come here as done
its said and done
don't you ever run
come here as done
because its said and done

The Silent Room

my mind is alive
but my senses haven't arrived
since that accident I can't be
oh please God forbid me

my life in this place is an illusion
messed up things in my mind that become scarred on my face
trying to pass my solution with a resolution
because of the people in this domicile that are unlike any race
in this place filled with hate I put up with ridicule and try to hide

my saddened future has awakened
to a place where I'm ripped apart for being a Johnson
and I begin to question myself
raised up feeling mind well shakened
I'm scared of the one who calls the shots and acts like an Adolph Hitler
I'm sinking in, well within inside my mind
oh please God forbid me from reaching this place
put me away
put me in the silent room

destruction and hate fills the room
I want to be left alone and I try to get through to you
this special room of doom
I try to get through to you

that I don't' need you and I wouldn't bother you
I feel like I'm getting this poison shoved down my lung
its like dead animals skin being made into a coat and being hung
you know I don't like you when I look at you
so why don't you leave me alone and do what you do
to someone else

the quiet room is for me
its not for you
nothing to do
that is for you
so pay your fee

my mind is alive
but my senses haven't arrived
since that accident I can't be
oh please God forbid me

my life in this place is an illusion
messed up things in my mind that become scarred on my face
trying to pass my solution with a resolution
because of the people in this domicile that are unlike any race
in this place filled with hate I put up with ridicule and try to hide

my saddened future has awakened
to a place where I'm ripped apart for being a Johnson
and I begin to question myself in this world
raised up feeling, my mind well shakened
I'm scared of the one who calls the shots and acts like Joseph Stalin
I'm sinking in, well within, inside my mind
oh please God forbid me from reaching this place
put me away
put me in the silent room

the quiet room is for me
its not for you
nothing to do
that is for you

so pay your fee

death's door has opened for me
nothing else is left for me
everything has hit me so hard
tired of the constant battles of humiliation
from my peers and the mounting taunts from teachers
of my past as well as the future with the world of high school
don't shed a tear for my love or my imagination
to be here I would rather enter the door of death
I can see myself walk into the big puddle of blood, but its a pool
the end will come for me and I'll swim in, away from the creatures
when will I be taken? you may ask, but you'll never know the continuation
why does this have to happen to me? because I don't like it here
I don't deserve this life of judgment from stupid kids at school
stupid kids that revolve their life and future around high school
you'll hear me laugh as I puke in their faces with disgust

my mind was alive
but my senses are dead
I'm floating away to the astral world
when will I arrive? I ask
my body was naked when I was born and I was kept fed
this physical world has hurt me so much that I don't want to live
but do I deserve to go into the after world? If it's a replay
of the life I just lived then I don't want to live
I don't want a replay

my saddened future has awakened
to a place where I'm ripped apart for being a Johnson
when there's thousands and millions of us, just look in the phone book
and I begin to question myself about the world around me
raised up feeling mind well shakened
I'm scared of the one who calls the shots and acts like Mao
I'm sinking in, well within, inside my mind
oh please God forbid me from reaching this place
put me away

Red Dragon Fantasy; Song Lyrics and Poetry

put me in the silent room

used to the idea in this silent room

enjoy the life in the silent room
and where you can enjoy the world of the silent room
together to make believe you're in control in the silent room

shoulder to shoulder you can laugh and shout in the silent room
here you can scream and cry in the silent room
inside a cube you won't have to worry about hurting yourself
together you'll have friends wearing white clothes
AND DIE

my mind was alive
and my senses were dead
when will I arrive?
my body to bare fed
this plane has hurt me to live
but deserve this much

my saddened future has awakened
to a place where I'm ripped apart for being a Johnson
when there's millions and trillions of us, just look in the phone book
soon you'll take back what you say about a Johnson and shut your mouth
I begin to question myself about the world around me
raised up feelings, my mind well shakened
I'm scared of the one who calls the shots and acts like our president
I'm sinking in, well within, inside my mind
oh please God forbid me from reaching this place
put me away
put me in the silent room

the quiet room is for me
its not for you
nothing to do
that is for you

so pay your fee

my mind is alive
but my senses haven't arrived
since that accident I can't be
oh please, God forgive me

Devastation

they say the human brain is like a computer
they say the human mind can tell the future
they say the human feelings can make people think
they say the human voice can make you blink
they say a person is bomb waiting to explode
and should be eliminated

there is this barren old might
that is hollow and dark as night
you can unleash your temper as simple as now
it can be silent as night, but end in a flash
turn around to face your maker and bow

we'll find out how it works
you can sit down and start lighting your smokes
you'll kill yourself if you don't release it
you can't see it
you can't believe it
the way it should've been
when you see how society is destroyed

devastation
I will devastate your life
devastation
let me demonstrate this life
devastation
demonstration
life as it seems I will devastate

do you know? how much blood has been spilled?
or do you realize? how man has created war to justify the common good
the pain and suffering of this here mother earth
can you see or are you blind?
you can't see, the encouraged sign
of the atom bomb being unleashed
and how a human race can break apart like leaves

devastation
I will devastate your life
devastation
let me demonstrate this life
devastation
demonstration
life as it seems I will devastate

this is lifeless   this is hell
this is pain   this is suffering
life has ended   society has fell
we've gone insane   gone relentless

so let me demonstrate   lets devastate
so let me demonstrate   lets devastate
so let me demonstrate   lets devastate
and we'll open those fucking eyes to the dangers of war

they say the human brain is like a computer
they say the human mind can tell the future
they say the human feelings can make people think
they say the human voice can make you blink
they say a person is bomb waiting to explode
and should be eliminated

I would like to see them eliminate people
who would die to have freedom

people like me who learned more education on their own than the
years of grade school junior high and high school combined.

devastation
I will devastate your life
devastation
let me demonstrate this life
devastation
demonstration
life as it seems I will devastate

Immortality

I'm not myself
I say this as I look in the mirrors
I'm changing myself
so I can blend in with my peers
but I'm left alone
I'm an immortal and I've grown old
the others of my kind are gone
they ran to the ends of the earth and their gone
I feel unique because of the things I've done
but there's no one that understands me
no one in this institution of knowledge

I see a girl walking down the hallway
and when I smile at her she give me a disgusting look
like I'm a devil worshiper and I forget to find my way
the girls in this institution aren't lady like, but live like whores
I'm an immortal who shall fall in love with a mortal girl who cares about the look
the look of how love should be and demonstrate it by the act of it through the core

me
me be mortal   *immortality*
I be mortal   *immortality*
me
me be mortal   *immortality*
I be mortal   *immortality*

immortality

me
me be mortal *immortality*
I be mortal *immortality*
me
me be mortal *immortality*
I be mortal *immortality*
Immortality

I've been changing within
strengthening within
growing within
something as once was shall be within

I have more strength than you, ten times the strength
of the mortal school boys I see here because that's all they are, boys
I have more life than you, including all the teenage whores
that lie in bed like a flipped hamburger on a grill
that lay there, spread open, waiting for a man
to go in and out,　　　　*to go in and out*

I'm stronger than all of you
younger than all of you
older than all of you
I have nothing in common with you

me
me be mortal *immortality*
I'll be mortal *immortality*
me
me be mortal *immortality*
I'll be mortal *immortality*
immortality

me
me be mortal *immortality*
I be mortal *immortality*

me
me be mortal *immortality*
I be mortal *immortality*
immortality

I'm living alone; me, myself, and I
I'm not used to this much solitude
I'm not used to so many idiots in this school that attend
that think their better than me? we shall see
because I'm immortal and I can live forever
how about you?

and then out of all this chaos I see her emerge from the darkness
and her name is Ariel and she is different
she's an immortal that understands me in every way and I hear what she has to say
we fit together so well and we're so perfect for each other in a sea that's so heartless
we'll be therefore each other forever no matter what the world has to say
because we're immortal twins in a school full of vampires
that hate anyone that is different

me
me be mortal *immortality*
I'll be mortal *immortality*
me
me be mortal *immortality*
I'll be mortal *immortality*
immortality

Agitation

"No, no you can't be that,"
"No, no you can't do that,"

agitation

agitation
agitation

agitation
agitation
agitation
like poison ivy
I'm going to make you itch until you bleed

can I come? can I come?
I want to go on ahead
and agitate you
I want to irritate you and drive you insane
your always doing it
making me hate myself and driving me insane
and you're always coming out ahead
so you better do
that's what you better do

how long do I have to sit in this fucking chair?
and where is the stupid teacher?
so I can get my awesome education
that my parents are paying out of their tax dollars
I'm taping my pencil and don't get this question
I don't understand this story problem or how to study
for tomorrow's English test, I think I'll just copy that dumb blonde's paper
because she's got all the answers for the questions

can I come? can I come?
I want to go on ahead
and agitate you, agitate the fuck out of you
I want to irritate you and drive you insane
your always doing it to me
class mates make me hate myself and drive me insane
and they're always coming out ahead until they graduate
so you better do   *that's right*
that's what you better do

before you graduate and carry that passion of putting people down
I'm sure the people you work with will love you for it

agitation
agitation
agitation

agitation
agitation
agitation
like poison ivy
I'm going to make you itch until you bleed

how long do I have to sit here in detention?
would it be possible to get a suspension or expelled?
because this education system sucks and blows like the wind
what our parents pay for is a prison that teaches kids how to hate
I'm with a selected few of trouble makers, who want attention
I see my sister, my immortal twin, and we give each other attention
she's there because she slammed the door into the teacher's head
I think its funny and I wish it was a few of my peers to get struck in the head
we think its funny; we scream and shout in the room because the teacher is out

how long do we have to sit in our desks and tap our pencils
in this awesome school with great education being taught
until we learn something that makes sense and survive
instead of having a teacher tell us what we can be when we grow up

"No no you can't be that" or " No No you can't do that" a teacher will tell us
"Mind your own fucking business" me and my sister hear them because they don't know our power and strengths.

"No, no you can't be that,"
"No, no you can't do that,"
we keep hearing them say in their agitating state

their mouth open up and down as they say it like a mindless puppet
and we sit and laugh while we say fuck you

can I come? can I come?
I want to go on ahead
and agitate you, agitate the fuck out of you
I want to irritate you and drive you insane
your always doing it to me
class mates make me hate myself and driving me insane
and they're always coming out ahead until they graduate
so you better do   *that's right*
that's what you better do
before you graduate and carry that passion of putting people down
I'm sure the people you work with will love you for it
and teachers can teach and pretend they know what they're doing

agitation
agitation
agitation

agitation
agitation
agitation
like poison ivy
I'm going to make you itch until you bleed

I think we'll stay home and teach ourselves
and avoid the stupid social activities
with my idiot class mates that think they're the star
and let the agitation continue its onslaught

Warm Envy

you woke up at night
to hear the cries that came from your childhood fright
too difficult to struggle
too hard to fight
and here you are eight years latter lying within yourself

too fragile like a child to admit to yourself
of the pain that you keep hidden within
you like to fight it and now its become brutal

can you feel the pain well inside
its like a knife being stabbed in your heart
oh tell me do you feel the way that I would feel?
when you hear that someone you loved has died
oh tell me can you feel the way I feel?
when a teacher called social services for the common good
oh do you feel the warm envy here?
of people who want what you have
and they don't care who they have to hurt to get it
do you feel the envy hidden within yourself
to have what other people have?

the pain is still inside of you
your walking around this school
this institution for education
with blood draining from your heart
how is it possible? what can you do?
and how do you keep going?
you walk around with this pain
with a step forward you set forth
and slowly your world eats at you and ends your worth
behind the stage of life, this place of after life
its so peaceful; its this spark of life inside you that interests me
can you hear my voice echo in your mind at this very night
you still live after this night
while others try to figure out how you do it
you're sick of the others gossip of your past
you do what must be done
so do it

now that you've witness the hate
of what has been done to you
what is it that you want to do?
they knife you for being a Jehovah Witness

they think its funny they think its offensive and disgusting
then they make you feel stupid in Hunters Safety
surprise, surprise when it was the instructor's fault
for telling you to turn around with the gun to the class

they knife you for making a mistake
they think its funny they think its offensive
and they'll spread rumors in school that you're so stupid
you pointed a loaded gun at the class and it won't go away for years

this bloody worth comes with agonizing tears
that is very destructive for a teenage boy
shall this come to pass? you'll have to wait and see
what will this envy do for you?
do you think you will get far?
sitting free without a sight of destructive criticism
this pain that you can't escape from five in the morning
to four in the evening
is like being in a torture chamber

can you feel the pain well inside
its like a knife being stabbed in your heart
oh tell me do you feel the way that I would feel?
when you hear that someone you loved has died
oh tell me can you feel the way I feel?
when a teacher called social services for the common good
oh do you feel the warm envy here?
of people who want what you have
and they don't care who they have to hurt to get it
do you feel the envy hidden within yourself
to have what other people have?

the image of the life you wanted
has to rise above you and do you feel happy?
why have they kept this from you?
and why do they continue with the taunting?
don't they like you?
this dreaded fear of a teenager to be accepted

your mind is scarred and memories emerge in your mind
of a child and what it was like to be innocent, free and loved
in this school, in this town, in this county, state and country

now that it has been done to you
what is it that you will do?
this bloody abuse worth shall come to pass
and what will this envy do to you?
do you think you will get far?
sitting free without a sight of your future
this pain consumes you and you can't escape

after you declare you're not a Jehovah Witness
they still sit and knife at you and say you worship the devil and "that Jesus is the Devil"
they spread rumors that your gay or they say you just admitted your gay
they also say its because you're a Johnson that's why things aren't done right
they say that a special bathroom has to be created for you
because you have male and female sex organ and everyone laughs
they spread rumors that your parents are brother and sister
and start their lawns on fire to collect insurance and create problems
and they think its funny when you get mad

they continue to knife you in the back by calling you a Jew
and laugh at you when you create your work of art "The Book"
and destroy it after all your hard work and put your through a depression.
you don't feel inclined to go to dances or have a desire to hang around anyone
from this school there is only the Nazis mind set of the master race
"the Jock, Prissy and Druggies" that tell you how it is and they continue to knife at you

you realize how disgusting this school is and how painful it is
to wake up every morning and sit in stagnation and a bully comes up
and punches you in the back while you're sitting, but don't worry it perfectly normal

because if you retaliate you'll get punished and told it takes two to tangle, period

nobody cares about you
almost nobody came to all your birthday parties or your graduation because they're envious of what you have
and what you can do, like ants attracted to a cup cake on the ground
especially when you take Hunters Safety a second time because you failed
you failed because the assholes distracted you from wanting to pass, they suck you dry
and the same instructor embarrassed you by saying how dumb you were for pointing the gun at the class when it was his fault to begin with and he laughs about it
he embarrassed you and helped ruin your life, what a joke, what a crock of shit
from that moment to the time you graduated
and while you graduated you can see everyone crying, wishing it could last forever
but you don't cry because you were happy to get out of the shit hole prison
and leave these sub-humans in the dust
and be happy to tell them to "shut the fuck up" when you see them later in life

can you feel the pain well inside
oh tell me do you feel the way I would feel
do you feel the envy hidden within here

the pain is still inside of you
your walking around this school
this institution for education
with blood draining from your heart
how is it possible? what can you do?
and how do you keep going?
you walk around with this pain
with a step forward you set forth
and slowly your world eats at you and ends your worth

behind the stage of life, this place of after life
its so peaceful; its this spark of life inside you that interests me
can you hear my voice echo in your mind at this very night
you still live after this night
while others try to figure out how you do it
you're sick of the others gossip of your past
you do what must be done
so do it

can you feel the pain well inside
its like a knife being stabbed in your heart
oh tell me do you feel the way that I would feel?
when you hear that someone you loved has died
oh tell me can you feel the way I feel?
when a teacher called social services for the common good
oh do you feel the warm envy here?
of people who want what you have
and they don't care who they have to hurt to get it
do you feel the envy hidden within yourself?
to have what other people have?

can you feel the pain well lit up inside?
oh tell me do you feel the way that I would feel?
oh tell me can you feel the way I can feel?
do you know this warm envy within here?
when you feel the warm envy
to steal another person's sacred flame
well inside and you make them feel that they want to die
then I'll say, you have the warm envy
and that you're nothing but a saddest

Private

feeling a lot of anger against my fellow class mates
feeling a lot disgust for my upper and lower class mates
I'm sick of the skanks and sluts picking on my sisters

I don't really care for any of my school work

why would I care when I can create my own world
with the stroke of my pencil and ignore the lecture

I'm so sick of this jock that I sit behind in Talkers class
he stinks of body odor, but he picks on kids for their body odor
I hate this jock in my grade, he's such a smart ass and he stinks
he likes to say faggot shit a lot and wears a black hat like a punk
he walks around like a tight ass with his fanny pack and reeks
he got his picture in the paper on graduation for an auto accident
and I wished he was killed in it and I don't feel bad for him
because he's buried shit and that's the truth

I'm feeling the incurred amount of hate when I stick up for my sister
the popular little bitch smart mouthed to me and I don't care who she is
I don't feel sorry for her when a rumor spreads around that I was window peeking
and it ruins her reputation and I shake my head in disgust when they believe it
stupid jocks and prissy bitches will believe everything they hear
and its pathetic when they don't follow the facts

I've taken enough of this bullshit
all of this hell, this school that's blazing fire,
this here hell, this external prison, a breeding ground
for teenage suicide or serial killers

I could see them getting knocked off, one by one
in a mental fuck down and disappear from society
I can hear them crying for their life and screaming for help
in this broken down choir, in this emotional suicide to the end
it has come near to me and near to them and the constant taunting
I hear from them

your nothing, your nobody - damage intake
your nothing, your nobody- damage intake
because your private and you're meant for nothing
your treated like your lower than dirt
and you can have a mental breakdown because its hell for you

and they like to say you're a dumb fuck and a mistake from God
your nothing, your nobody - damage intake
your nothing, your nobody - damage intake
because you're private and you're meant for nothing at all
your treated like your lower than dirt
and you can have a mental breakdown because its hell for you
and they like to say you're a dumb fuck and a mistake from God
your nothing, your nobody - damage intake
your nothing, your nobody - damage intake
so private, look at yourself - stay by yourself
because you don't have any friends

I'm in my desk and mind my own business
and a jock throws spit balls at me
I tell him to stop it, but he gives me a stupid smile
and continues to antagonize me
then I snap and get my adrenaline rush
I get up and start punching his head as hard as I can
I'm wearing my class ring and feel my fist
hit him in the back of the head and it feels so good
and my left fist hits him in the face and that feels even better

I'm feel hungry and want to go after the
other two stupid jocks who antagonize me
but then I get called to the office to be suspended
I feel so much power after that incident
I get respect and left the fuck alone, its so great
and none of the teachers did anything to prevent it
or stop me while I was punching the jock in the face
but then there's the stupid popular girls
who still believe the rumors of me window peeking
when I didn't

I can't say I feel sorry for them
I feel like they deserve all the back lash of hate
the world gives them
especially from the popular jock who tells
little kids that special Ed students are insane

as if he's so much better, yeah ok
he won't go anywhere in the future
in his short sighted future

I can see the concessions are here to stay
and are your own infection to save face
connections to move up in the world will limit you
can the druggies find the right connection to be on top?
uh huh druggies don't go anywhere unless they flunk
and stay in high school
uh huh and the prissy popular girls will work for seven dollars an hour
and still think their popular in their heads

the misery strikes me hard
when I realize I've been cheated out of my experiences
all that it was that I wanted is gone forever
am I'm torn apart to ride when I try to lose the fear
will I bust apart for being on trial for my small mistakes?
I lay down because I'm no longer the same person
I'm done with this fucking school and I'm so out of here
I paced myself and bottled my anger hoping I wouldn't blow
and it blew up in their fucking faces and I can still hear them say it

your nothing, your nobody - damage intake
your nothing, your nobody - damage intake
because your private and you're meant for nothing
your treated like your lower than dirt
and you can have a mental breakdown because its hell for you
and they like to say your a dumb fuck and a mistake from God
your nothing, your nobody - damage intake
your nothing, your nobody - damage intake
because you're private and you're meant for nothing at all
your treated like your lower than dirt
and you can have a mental breakdown because its hell for you
and they like to say you're a dumb fuck and a mistake from God
your nothing, your nobody - damage intake
your nothing, your nobody - damage intake
so private, look at yourself - stay by yourself

Red Dragon Fantasy; Song Lyrics and Poetry

because you don't have any friends

I like to mind my own business and write my stories
and draw my pretty little pictures
when this short little dude, comes up to me
to say this girl likes me, yeah ok
I don't realize that this short stubby little boy
is a small minded, scummy little insect that should be stepped on
but I'm naive and believe him and try to talk to her
he's the same little elf that picks a fight with me at a graduation party
and makes himself look like an ass, stupid wanna be jock, ass wipe
before I can talk to this girl, a jock starts walking with her like a dog
I put a rose in her locker and smile, thinking what a nice start for a friendship
and end up in the principals' office
the principle is such a dip shit
that I don't even know why he's wasting my time
he tells me that she liked the rose, but isn't interested in me
I walk out angry thinking what a bitch
and pissed at the stubby little dude
and the dumb ass principal for wasting my time
and I think to myself what a waste of my time

I find a letter written with girl's hand writing
and it says I've got a thick skull
and tells me how stupid I am for trying to go out
with that girl I gave the rose too
I decide to move on from this screwed up school
of stupid jocks, prissy plastic girls,
insects and dip-shit principle,
but I can hear them say negative things towards me

your nothing, your nobody - damage intake
your nothing, your nobody- damage intake
because your private and you're meant for nothing
your treated like your lower than dirt
and you can have a mental breakdown because its hell for you
and they like to say you're a dumb fuck and a mistake from God

your nothing, your nobody - damage intake
your nothing, your nobody - damage intake
because you're private and you're meant for nothing at all
your treated like your lower than dirt
and you can have a mental breakdown because its hell for you
and they like to say you're a dumb fuck and a mistake from God
your nothing, your nobody - damage intake
your nothing, your nobody - damage intake
so private, look at yourself - stay by yourself
because you don't have any friends

Bring It On

I've been waiting for you
I've been determined by you
I've felt destructive and you can't stop me
so you better break it off and leave me alone
they'll sit and laugh when they watch what they see
they're comfortable in their perfect home
like a parasite that burrows in a host

they do me damage emotionally and ruin my reputation
they act like I'm evil and that I'm the bad guy
when they're the ones who do the antagonizing
and they feel its their destiny to destroy my reputation
for life in this puke school, I count the days to graduation
you thought you could take me, but you failed and you know why
but its not enough because you have to tell everyone
that it was an act and that you're a real champ
but your nothing but a chump
and you like to lie
to save your life
and take as much as possible from everyone
because you're a liar and so are your scummy Jock friends

you could bring it on
when other teenagers call you a pussy
you could bring it on

when your team mates look down on you
you could bring it on
when your jock friendships end and its on you
you could bring it on
but you did it to yourself
and you got me mad

I shake my head when I hear these words
and think you're stupid because you are

bring it on
do you want to go right now?
bring it on
do you really think you can take me on ?
bring it on
salvage your wrong doing to this moment for now
are you simply ready for me

in a fight you will be done
bring it on
in a fight after school, I would have won
bring it on
in a fight seriously captured for you
bring it on
in a life there will be nothing left for you
bring it on
and then we'll see who wins

it is this time I feel threatened
he's got all his Jock buddies behind him
to save his reputation as a Jock and make him feel important
but all he is, is a big fucken joke
I can feel hell's fire stir as he speaks
I feel scarred and possessed by evil
I don't want to get into another fight
but I feel a thirst to beat the shit out of this Jock
I crave it like a drug addict desires cocaine or Meth
and I hear the little voice in my head

do you just want to end it right now?

you could bring it on
when other teenagers call you a pussy
you could bring it on
when your team mates look down on you
you could bring it on
when your jock friendships end and its on you
you could bring it on
but you did it to yourself
and you got me mad

I shake my head when I hear these words
and think you're stupid because you are

bring it on
do you want to go right now?
bring it on
do you really think you can take me on?
bring it on
salvage your wrong doing to this moment for now
are you simply ready for me?

in a fight you will be done
bring it on
in a fight after school, I would have won
bring it on
in a fight seriously captured for you
bring it on
in a life there will be nothing left for you
bring it on
and then we'll see who wins

playing games	you know	fame and glory
playing with fire	you know	its your story
feelings in range	they will	possess over
you		
cry for your needs	they should	be in place

bring it on
do you want to go right now?
bring it on
do you really think you can take me?
bring it on
salvage your wrong doing to this moment for now
are you simply ready for me?

Morale

come out here I hear him say
its the last spoken word today
come here he demands
and that's his last spoken word
before the big fight
you may think you might have me in sight
and get me chilling in my shoes with your words
I just want you to leave me
and I have to pay to be free
and I feel you must never return

you just think what you want to think
and I'll think about you the way I want to think
that you think can defeat me   now
because you can't beat me
and you know you can't defeat me
and you know it
and if that's not it then go ahead
you can hit me and you can kick me
but in the end you're mine

I have a stormed out feeling
that's strong enough for the fight
I can see the pierced ears on their ears, the earrings made of metal
its buried in my sight
the bullies are my height with the leader as tall as the ceiling
I can feel my blood turn to ice as I wait for what will happen next

steaming up motion
mind driven off course
feminine in notion
cracked open scabs reveals the sores

you just think what you want to think
and I'll think about you the way I want to think
that you think can defeat me   now
because you can't beat me
and you know you can't defeat me
and you know it
and if that's not it then go ahead
you can hit me and you can kick me
but in the end you're mine

I can feel the beating in my life
you can beat as much as you can
and as much as you want
but at the end you are mine
after you have had your fun
you will soon learn my dear fun
because you know you can't beat me
and you better watch you back right now
you better watch your back for now
because I'm invincible

you just think what you want to think
and I'll think about you the way I want to think
that you think can defeat me   now
because you can't beat me
and you know you can't defeat me
and you know it
and if that's not it then go ahead
you can hit me and you can kick me
but in the end you're mine

Dooms Day Paper Mesh-a

I'm your dooms day paper mesh-a
I'm your attitude problem fucken -a
I'm your dooms day paper mesh-a
don't screw with me fucken -a
I've got a dooms day paper mesh-a
you got an attitude problem turducken-a
I've got dooms day paper mesh-a
don't screw with me fucken -a

ha, *ha*
how are ya doing?
nobody ya fooling
juggling at the tips of your life
be careful doing the things you aren't
doing what shouldn't be one
fooling around and thinking your cool
of course its the idiots who think they rule
just remember this to the end

I'm your dooms day paper mesh-a
I'm your attitude problem fucken -a
I'm your dooms day paper mesh-a
don't screw with me fucken -a
I've got a dooms day paper mesh-a
you got an attitude problem fucken-a
I've got dooms day paper mesh-a
don't screw with me fucken -a

living every day you know unend
not knowing
unknowing
annoying
life as ending as the dooms day
don't miss judge for you will pay

I'll create a work of art out paper mesh-a

it could be a knife made of paper
or a gun that I can point at your head
a dragon or dinosaur that's hungry
for juicy jocks and preppy bitches
with asshole wannabe and popular kids
I could make a life sized coffin out of paper mesh-a
so you can be buried alive under the dirt
 you can see its as easy as paper mesh-a

I'm your dooms day paper mesh-a
I'm your attitude problem fucken -a
I'm your dooms day paper mesh a
don't screw with me fucken -a
I've got a dooms day paper mesh-a
you got an attitude problem fucken-a
I've got dooms day paper mesh-a
don't screw with me fucken -a

easily as paper
I crumble apart coming and forging
back into paper mesh-a
strictly the end of you draws closer
start begging more, you simpleton poser
dowse of rain for the end of pain

I'll wrap you up in paper mesh-a
and listen to you scream in fear
I'll get a chain saw and cut off your arms
I'll get my grandpa's gun
and use you as target practice
there will be blood all over the floor
but then I'll re-attach your arms from the paper mesh-a

I'm your dooms day paper mesh-a
I'm your attitude problem fucken -a
I'm your dooms day paper mesh-a
don't screw with me fucken -a
I've got a dooms day paper mesh-a

you got an attitude problem fucken -a
I've got dooms day paper mesh-a
don't screw with me fucken -a

serious little crimes draw near
crowding little children in crazed fear
looking at the small accidents of planet earth
because after this hell, there shall be no rebirth

watch as I rip the paper in half
to retell the song of my paper mesh-a
and how I feel about the humanoids
I went to school with

I'm your dooms day paper mesh-a   a dooms day paper
mesh -a
I'm your attitude problem fucken -a   people have attitude
problems fucken-a
I'm your dooms day paper mesh-a   a dooms day paper
mesh-a
don't screw with me fucken -a   authority wipe your attitude
fucken-a
I've got a dooms day paper mesh-a   a dooms day paper
mesh-a
you got an attitude problem fucken-a   your school psychologist will
fucken say
I've got dooms day paper mesh-a   dooms day paper mesh-a
don't screw with me fucken -a   you got an attitude problem
fucken-a

Heart Of Hell II

extravagant as it seems
for I have no open heart
high wall and beams
for now they will fall apart

in this world of school
I'm waiting for someone to plant a bomb
so that it can blow up the school
and then all my hardships will go away
the teachers don't know what goes on
especially when a student gets harassed everyday

its a heart of hell
when a teacher teaches what their told
its a heart of hell
when the principle punishes the innocent
its a heart of hell
when nobody cares about bully jocks
treat the student like crap

heart of hell
there's no love for you today
hard as hell
deadly games I will do for play
heart of hell
stay out for you've entered a heart of hell

yes I know I've heard these stories before
grade school teachers will prey on your mind
jocks only care about themselves and run for the door
there's no time to beg no expectation for apology or to be kind
displease me if you will, you can stop over to make your kill
you may want to stop this horrid habit that you want to fulfill

its a heart of hell
when a teacher teaches what their told
its a heart of hell
when the principle punishes the innocent
its a heart of hell
when nobody cares about bully jocks
treat the student like crap

heart of hell

there's no love for you today
hard as hell
deadly games I will do for play
heart of hell
stay out for you've entered a heart of hell

something's not right
there's nothing good about tonight
I hear the gossiping bullshit of upper and lower classman
talk about students when they're the ones who shouldn't talk
its like a dragon slayer who is a jock looking for a dragon in smog
before he realizes it, the red dragon emerges and eats him like a hog

its a heart of hell
when a teacher teaches what their told
its a heart of hell
when the principle punishes the innocent
its a heart of hell
when nobody cares about bully jocks
treat the student like crap

heart of hell
there's no love for you today
hard as hell
deadly games I will do for play
heart of hell
stay out for you've entered a heart of hell

This Magical Place

Mind Shut Your Mouth
You're The Secret
She Could Have Been You
Sugar Baby
This Magical Place
Since I don't Have You
Without You
We're Hot And You're Not
Its All My Fault
Wolves Of Justice
Eagle In My Light
You're The Secret II

Mind Shut Your Mouth

every time I speak
I feel like I'm climbing a mountain to its peak
you don't know me and I don't know you
but there's no reason why we can't be together
this doesn't seem real to me
and this doesn't seem real to you
but if you give it a chance you will find a world for us forever
a world together that you will hear that I have big loud mind

can you see me looking at you from across the room
you're in Truffle and Jersey's class looking so fancy in your desk
I'm not paying attention to what the teachers are lecturing
because I'm thinking about how good we would be together
I'm not high with these thoughts and I know my heart is true
I may be quiet, but my thoughts are louder than the rest
I'm reading your lips while the teacher is lecturing
because I'm thinking about us being together sooner or latter

mind shut your mouth
because I don't need ya
just shut your mouth
mind shut your mouth
because I can't see ya
mind just shut your mouth

every time that I speak I feel like I'm climbing a mountain to its peak
I'm thinking about how I want to kiss you in front of everyone
I'm thinking how I want to make out with you and make everyone freak
I think you would find it fun and think I would be funner than anyone
we could make out in Truffle and Jersey's class
and enjoy teaching each other in Talker and Black's class
can you feel the electricity in the air ? and we'll be here at last
I need,   I need you as much as you need me
a world together that you will hear that I have big loud mind
because I'm thinking about us being together sooner or latter

mind shut your mouth
because I don't need ya
just shut your mouth

mind shut your mouth
because I can't see ya
mind just shut your mouth

I'll be your student today
and tomorrow I'll be your teacher
you can help me with my math
and I'll teach you how to play
can you feel the day move in fast forward, it moves faster
and when I look at you I'll know where you're at

mind shut your mouth
mind shut your mouth
because I don't' need ya
just shut your mouth
mind shut your mouth
because I don't need ya
just shut your mouth

You're The Secret (The Original)

you're the secret
so mysterious
so of it

you're the secret that has no ending
and no beginning
s
you're so wondrous   to my eyes
you're so serious   to my eyes

hiding from place to place
I don't know what there is to expect

whatever is hidden within your face
passion and respect
yet I do know you're a secret
you're the secret

you're the secret
so mysterious
so of it

you're the secret
that has no ending
and no beginning
to what extent

I don't know what the secret is
not yet anyways, about you
everything that I've experienced seems so new
I don't know how to express it, but I'll find out what it is

you're so wondrous
you're so passionate
you're so drawn for attention
and you've got my affection

you're the secret
that I know
I found it interesting

I like to watch you laugh
I feel excited and I get embarrassed and turn red
as much as me
I find out what it is, as it is said

you're the secret
I don't know what the secret is
about you
but I'll find it within you

She Could've Been You

I'm missing you
and I wanted to know more about you
and I wanted to be your sweet heart
but like so many hardships before
I can feel my chest hurt with a broken heart
for some reason I feel like I had it coming
I'm on my way out, I'm running out the door

I wanted to love you
for a reason that boys and girls do
they don't let go
unless they stay far away
if it hurts so much
then I won't touch you again
until you're ok

she could've been you
and I can see your face emerge from the water
she could've been, all of you
and I can see your face emerge from the fire
she could've been you, all of you

she could've been you, all of you
I want you to be her, all of her
to step out from the shadows, emerge from the darkness
I want you to be her, all of her
to step out of my dreams from the bright sun
she could've been you, all of you
and I want you to be her, all of her

I'm missing you
and I wanted to know more, but there's nothing I can do
I'm crying in tears and I'm falling apart
my heart is broken, its shattered to the core
when I see your face I can feel my broken heart
I try so hard and love is no work of art

I'm on my way out, I'm running out the door

she could have been you, all of you
I want you to be her, all of her
to step out from the shadows, emerge from the darkness
I want you to be her, all of her
to step out of my dreams from the bright sun
she could have been you, all of you
and I want you to be her, all of her

I look in your eyes and see all of your lies
why is the pain so real?
it cuts like knives and I'm bleeding
when it rains will it heal?

I wanted to love you
for the reason that boys and girls do
they don't let go
unless they stay far away
if it hurts so much
then I won't touch you again
until you're ok

she could've been you
and I can see your face emerge from the water
she could've been, all of you
and I can see your face emerge from the fire
she could've been you, all of you

she could've been you, all of you *the water* I want you to be her, all of her to step out from the shadows, emerge from the darkness *the fire* I want you to be her, all of her to step out of my dreams	*her face emerge from* *her face emerges from*

from the big bright sun   *her face emerges from the*
water
she could've been you, all of you
and I want you to be her, all of her   *her face emerges from*
the fire

Sugar Baby

this is too much
for me to endure
this is too much
for me to cure

its eleven o'clock, an hour before midnight
I'm in my little desk, in my little room
I'm busy writing and creating my world of light
I'm thinking of you baby and there's plenty of room

with every stroke of my pencil I can see your face
with movement of caffeine and sugar shoved in my face
makes my mind move faster and faster, like a race
its like a case of sugar and speed that quickens the pace

to put up with you I would need to be with you
creativity and love has been unleashed, which is true
there's too much sugar in my system
I've got a light headed message drawn too dim

you can be my sugar baby
sugar baby
you can be my sugar baby
sugar baby
you can be my sugar baby
and we can party all night in my world

I can see your face in my dreams
I can draw your face in my fantasy
with every stroke of my pencil, you can be the girl of my dreams

and the nights we spend I'll feel like I'm on ecstasy
when I see you smile you make my mind move faster and faster

to put up with you I would need to be with you
creativity and love has been unleashed, which is true
there's too much sugar in my system
I've got a light headed message drawn too dim

you can be my sugar baby
sugar baby
you can be my sugar baby
sugar baby
you can be my sugar baby
and we can party all night in my world

its one minute to midnight and I'm almost finished
its going to end tonight with the last page and then I'm finished
I'm almost done creating you on paper and then you'll be finished

I can see your face in my dreams   *and I want you in my dreams*
I can draw your face in my fantasy   *and I want it to be a reality*
with every stroke of my pencil, you can be the girl of my dreams,
    a beautiful dream
and the nights we spend I'll feel like I'm on ecstasy,
    and it gives me elasticity
when I see you smile, you make my mind move faster and faster
    faster and faster

you can be my sugar baby
sugar baby   *be my sugar baby*
you can be my sugar baby
sugar baby   *be my sugar baby*
you can be my sugar baby
and we can party all night in my world
you can be my sugar baby
sugar baby   *be my sugar baby*
you can be my sugar baby
sugar baby   *be my sugar baby*

you can be my sugar baby
and we can party all night in my world
sugar baby   *be my sugar baby*

This Magical Place

I look around and watch our inheritance
being born every second of the day
I can see the beginning of a rose coming up from the ground
can you see the birth of a new animal coming your way?
can you hear the call of tiger, its an amazing sound?
we as humans can survive and see the importance
of what the world needs, to keep the balance

some people say we live in a magical world
the world gives us what we need, the forgiving seed
more than a million species live in the ocean, a magical world
more energy in the magnetic field than we know what to do with
more secrets than we know exist that could help instead
in this magical place

because we're living in a magical place
its just as plain as it is on my face
because we're living in a magical world
won't you just stop, there's nothing to worry
because we're living in this magical place

you can watch a rose unfolding
its amazing and very unraveling
stand with me and watch the aurora shining
and you can see the start of a new species coming
the earth heals itself and you'll want to be loving
so come now and step into this magical place

because we're living in a magical place
its just as plain as it is on my face
because we're living in a magical world
won't you just stop, there's no worry

because we're living in this magical place

you can see how powerful our world is
you can hear how wonderful the world is
you can smell how delicious the world is
you can feel the strength the world is
because its a magical world

because we're living in a magical place
its just as plain as it is on my face
because we're living in a magical world
won't you just stop, there's no worry
because we're living in this magical place

this magical place
this magical place

because we are living in a magical place
because we are loving this magical place
we're living and growing in this magical place

magical world
magical world

how can we survive when we criticize other racism
look in my eyes until you see my face

magical magical
magical magical
this magical place

because we're living
and growing
and saving each other
in this magical world

this magical place
this magical place

this magical place

because we're living in a magical place
its just as plain as it is on my face
because we're living in a magical world
won't you just stop, there's no worry
because we're living in this magical place

this magical place
this magical place
this magical place

Since I Can't Have You

since your gone   since I lost you
sensible reason   gone of hand
loss of interest   love to do
buried to me   why is it this way?

I've worked so hard to get your attention
I've been working overtime to get your affection
it seems like there is no hope for this friendship
it feels like the eclipse of the sun and there is no relationship
the kids in this school don't want us together
they laugh and think its funny when I think about us forever

I want to be with you forever, but the kids in the school don't like it
its because I'm a Johnson and I could grow up being better than them
they think I'm pathetic if I buy you roses for valentine's day and you like it
sometimes I wish I was in a different school with you so that I could win
since I can't have you

since I can't have you
I feel my heart trembling in pain
since I can't have you
I feel my face shake with frustration

since I don't have you
I feel my heart shatter as I go insane
since I don't have you
I lower my head in resignation

oh
since I can't have you
oh oh
since I can't have you
oh
since I don't have you
oh oh
since I don't have you

I've worked so hard to get your affection
I've been busting my ass to get your attraction
it seems like there is no hope for us and I watch you walk away
I'm so sad with a lot of anger and I don't know what to say
the kids in this school don't want us together
they laugh and think its funny when I think about us forever

since I can't have you
I feel my heart trembling in pain
since I can't have you
I feel my face shake with frustration
since I don't have you
I feel my heart shatter as I go insane
since I don't have you
I lower my head in resignation

oh
since I can't have you
oh oh
since I can't have you
oh
since I don't have you
oh oh
since I don't have you

In my dreams, I move my head back and forth
I'm thrashing in my nightmares because I have no worth
I feel like you've left me and I'm feeling really weak
I'm on a boat and it has a broken seal

I gave you a rose
and you gave me a heart break
and I'm expected to seal the leak

oh
since I can't have you
oh oh
since I can't have you
oh
since I don't have you
oh oh
since I don't have you
oh
since I can't have you
oh oh
since I can't have you

Without you

when I fall asleep
I think about you
there is no one else but you
and the thoughts persist
of what I'd like to do with you

when I was with you
I felt well and powerful
and not alone
when I was with you
I felt I knew, when I talked to you on the phone
since forever I knew you

and baby it was wonderful

without you
I'm too alone
shame full eyes have adapted and rise
without you
I feel undone
eyes of hope and we shall became wise
without you
I feel alone
my heart beats faster with what love does
without you

in time
or the wrong time
I think of you, I think about you   *all the time*
my eyes lower down when I see you frown
and see your down, without me
without you

I can't wait to see you
to see you in front of me
in front of me kissing my lips and my heart flutters
it flutters like a bird is in my chest begging for more
from you

without you
I'm too alone
shame full eyes have adapted and rise
without you
I feel undone
eyes of hope and we shall became wise
without you
I feel alone
my heart beats faster with what love does
without you

We're Hot and Your Not

we're going to rock this game
we're going to knock you down
kick you all the way
we'll make sure you rot
all the way home

because we're hot and you're not
this is our Spartan theme
because we're hot and you're not
that's our Spartan theme

prepare, prepare to get kicked in the face
to get stomped by all
to be beaten by us
there's no pity for you

because we're hot and you're not
this is our Spartan theme
because we're hot and you're not
that's our Spartan theme

we beat you   we won
we knocked you off
that was our task

because we're hot and you're not
this is our Spartan theme
because we're hot and you're not
that's our Spartan theme

we killed the pigs
slaughter them whole
surrounded them to beat them
that's the Spartan theme

because we're hot and you're not
this is our Spartan theme

because we're hot and you're not
that's our Spartan theme

Its All My Fault

my mind is at a hunted fault
my thought at a dreaded insult
she shamed me for ignorance
and we got into a dreaded fight
but then that night I remember
when she had gotten into that accident

I feel so guilty for what I said
I wish I kept her close instead
but now all that's left are these feelings
these emotions that won't give me these healings

its all my fault
I can hear my voice break
its all my fault
I can feel my heart break
its all my fault
I can see my soul break
its all my fault

its all my fault
its all my fault
its all my fault

in fear I went to her
to save her, to be the first with her
all my chances and dreams became lost
lost love was crushed and so was I
she had no change of consciousness and was dead
I sat in tears with darkness around me as they pushed me away
I screamed and shouted her name as I unleashed my fight
and pushed her away to her grave
and I can hear my parents say

its all your fault
I can hear my voice break
its all your fault
I can feel my heart break
its all your fault
I can see my soul break
its all your fault

its all your fault
its all your fault
its all your fault
its all your fault
its all your fault
its all your fault

on that dark Sunday morning
I look at her grave to put down some flowers
I'm standing here trying to be brave, but I'm not brave
but there's something I wanted to say
that it wasn't given did not seem to last
because its all my fault

its all my fault
I can hear my voice break
its all my fault
I can feel my heart break
its all my fault
I can see my soul break
its all my fault

its all my fault
its all my fault
its all my fault

I hear the world yell to me

its all your fault

its all your fault
its all your fault

its all my fault
its all my fault
its all my fault

Wolves of Justice

looking pack of the past
never lasting they are the pack
sharpening their claws
awaiting for the evil black shroud
hiding up above, the ceiling they go
they, they'll stay until they know
these wolves are stronger than you realize

are you paralyzed? because off they go
characterized as outsiders, there they go
you can't determine who's side there on
off to the legend that you will know

are you flying out in the star lit sky?
start running in the deadly city where you may die
they'll search you out, they'll hunt down the guilty
out to get justice, they will

paralyzed off they go
characterized there they go
you can't determine their side
off to the name and meaning you will know

shifting on out into the midnight air
evil from hell they will fight
Sasha Lone Wolf at their side
he awaits, sharpening his deadly gauntlets
within the deep alleys there they are

only one has a loaded gun
he, he feels
one power stick deepens the wounds of the past
congratulations for defeating the dragons
for you know he is as smart and sly
he holds the sword of power, and will swing the blade

looking back into the past
everlasting, but they are the last
they are our heroes and they stand proud
they'll wait for Tora Slash to come out from the shadows
they'll come out from hiding in the shadows
and they'll stand to lend a helping hand and it shows
these wolves are stronger than you realize

paralyzed off they go
characterized there they go
you can't determine their side
off to the legend that you will know

shifting on out into the midnight air
evil from hell they will fight
Sasha Lone Wolf at their side
he awaits, sharpening his deadly gauntlets
within the deep alleys there they are
only one has a loaded gun
he, he feels
one power stick deepens the wounds of the past
congratulations for defeating the dragons
for you know he is as smart and sly
he holds the sword of power, and will swing the blade

there's something that doesn't seem right
when there's nothing to do, but fight
I sense an enemy is one of us
when my blade swings strong and long to the east
and I discover it is thyself who can save us

paralyzed off they go
characterized there they go
you can't determine their side
off to the legend for The Wolves of Justice

The Eagle In My Light

I saw my string of fate
its the sorrow that surrounds me
as darkness surrounds you
when you turn off the light
broken promise, shattered trust
I couldn't let it happen again,   *I won't let it happen again*
I would have to over protect myself
to keep myself away from the pain
the hurt and the feeling of guilt could consume me again
it falls on my face like the rain
with it, I struggle without you

there has been so many hardships
that there is too struggle alone with
I never wanted to think I needed you
for the love that you've shown
as the eagle in my light

there has been so much pain that I've had to feel
I can feel the tears fall on my cheeks as I heal
I didn't think I could have you
for the love you gave me
as the eagle in my light

to the harsh degree of hurt I felt
you helped me overcome them
and I see a whole new light, a whole new world
although, I have thought not to use this power
that you gave me to heal the world
the evil in this domain of soulless sinners

I knew I needed it this power that binds
like a friend of friends, a person that needs friends
or a person who has friends and gets betrayed
I never wanted to believe that I needed you

there has been so many hardships
that there is too struggle alone with
I never wanted to think I needed you
for the love that you've shown
as the eagle in my light

there has been so much pain that I've had to feel
I can feel the tears fall on my cheeks as I heal
I didn't think I could have you
for the love you gave me
as the eagle in my light

I look around to see everything is in ruin
there is smoldering smoke and the foundation is burnt
everything is gone and my childhood is in ruin
is there hope for me to rebuild? even when everything is burnt
what has fallen could never be
and then the sun shines and an eagle lands
because of you I dreamed things could never be
they could never be
they can only be better
as the eagle in my light

there has been so many hardships
that there is too struggle alone with
I never wanted to think I needed you
for the love you've shown
as the eagle in my light

there has been so much pain that I've had to feel
I can feel the tears fall on my cheeks as I heal
I didn't think I could have you
for the love you gave me

as the eagle in my light

You're The Secret II

I see you're not the average girl
I see you sitting next to me in class

I get shivers when I see she's like a pearl
she makes me want her and I can't stay on task
she's the secret

I go to my locker after class
I turn my head and I see her at last
she's so beautiful, the way she parts her hair
I'm in a dumpy school and a crappy class
and life seems so unfair
if I was like the cool kids she would be a blast

you're the secret
so mysterious
so of it
you're the secret
that has no ending
and no beginning
you're the secret
so fictitious
like the anima
banging on my door
a secret key to my world
you're the secret

you're the secret
you're so wondrous   to my eyes
you're so serious   to my eyes
I want you to like me   so don't listen to the lies
I want you to want me   can you hear my cries?
you're the secret

I see you're not an average girl
I see you're standing in front of me in the hallway
I can smell your perfume and your hair spray
I look at you when you look at me and it blows me away
you start to smile at me and I can see you're an extraordinary girl
I want to make love with you right now in the commons because you're my pearl
and all the cool kids can sit and watch us because they would be blown away

you're the secret
so mysterious
so of it
you're the secret
that has no ending
and no beginning
you're the secret
so fictitious
like the anima
banging on my door
a secret key to my world
you're the secret

you're the secret
you're so wondrous   to my eyes
you're so serious   to my eyes
I want you to like me   so don't listen to the lies
I want you to want me   can you hear my cries?
you're the secret

they don't know what the secret is about you
not yet anyways, about you
everything that I want to experience
with you will seem so new and I want to carry
I don't know how to express it,
 but I'll find out more about it this February

you're the secret

so mysterious
so of it
you're the secret
hat has no ending
and no beginning
you're the secret
so fictitious
like the anima
banging on my door
a secret key to my world
you're the secret

you're the secret
you're so wondrous   to my eyes
you're so serious   to my eyes
I want you to like me   so don't listen to the lies
I want you to want me   can you hear my cries?
 you're the secret

Thunder Road Forever

Thunder Road Forever
Agenda For Forever
Eve's Garden
Symphony For Sympathy
Madness
Fadedness
Attack Force
Deep Fur
I Don't Care
Ain't So Bad After All
Splintered Sliver
Taking Control
Music In My Head
Brain Storming
Blue Soundra
Language Of Love

Thunder Road Forever

they say that paradise is just like this
people know what it is when it seems so right
we can keep walking on a golden road with flowers
rain or sunshine on and on with long green towers
do you know what this remind me of?
I can't believe what this reminds me of

can you see?
this is just like the thunder road
forever and ever and ever I see
can you see?
this is just like the thunder road
forever and ever and ever I see
can you see?
this is just like the thunder road
forever and ever and ever I see

plant yourself a goodnight rest
lay yourself from all the stress, in full nights
      all the stress, in full nights
lay down and forget about yesterday's mess
just forget about the violence and the fight
did you know you entered the world
where beauty circles you around and around
wide and bright huge but small, like a pearl
and it makes you think about the world

can you see?
this is just like the thunder road
forever and ever and ever I see
can you see?
this is just like the thunder road
forever and ever and ever I see
can you see?
this is just like the thunder road

forever and ever and ever I see

happiness and glory seeps through your mind
it shakes the worries and doom that you may find
doom that you may find
they're glories and wonderful, it must be just like thunder road
thunder road forever, is a wonderful paradise
the ground starts to shake and rattle
rambunctious and bright as I hold
and jump back in the saddle

can you see?
this is just like the thunder road
forever and ever and ever I see
can you see?
this is just like the thunder road
forever and ever and ever I see
can you see?
this is just like the thunder road
forever and ever and ever I see

Agenda For Forever

painstaking, they say is forever
favoritism of people, they say is forever
choices they make whenever
for any kind of treasure
oh baby do you know what I'm saying?
lost loves, lost like a rose
I hear them crying, I hear them shouting
I'll try to find you
which is the thing to do, for you?

in this world there's a loving world of love
men and women hold each other when they're in love
its this world that I see the people around me
their lying in the sun and its real fun to see

these people are making love and having fun
I look up and smile as I see the golden sun

do you know? do you know?
the agenda for forever
do you know? do you know?
to not hold a grudge forever
do you know? do you know?
the agenda for forever

do you know our future?
when you look into our picture?
I see forever
do you see? do you see?
trust
that is, if you dare
to hurt me
for you I hope is rare

do you know where we are?
how is it that we can get along so well
in magical bliss, in paradise that's where we are
I can see a world of peace and everything is well
I look around and see everything is won
I cross my arms and smile as I see the golden sun

do you know? do you know?
the agenda for forever
do you know? do you know?
to not hold a sin forever
do you know? do you know?
the agenda for forever

I hope you know, I hope you know
the agenda for forever
because its here with us in forever
do you know? do you know?
the agenda for forever

do you know? do you know?
the agenda for forever
do you know? do you know?
to not hold a grudge forever
do you know? do you know?
the agenda for forever

Eve's Garden

there's a place that I know
and its name is eve's garden
where Haiti can never come to wreck the beauty
so come on sweetie

there's a place that I go
where we escape the burden
where we never age or die
and when your there you'll know why

let's get ready
let's get ready
all you know   *anything you want to show*
no stress, no worry   *and don't need to say sorry*
no apologies needed, no need to say sorry
all you know   *anything you want to show*
no stress, no worry   *and don't need to say sorry*
no apologies needed, no need to say sorry
all you want to have   *is there before you*
all you need to have   *is everything before you*
just remember the condition

no more talking snakes
no more talking snakes
no more burning tree
no more eating the fee

its the price you pay when living in the garden

the price you lose when you steal from the garden
the damage you do which will cause you to age
false believers shall leave the garden
and they will die of old age
just turn the page

let's get ready
let's get ready
all you know   *anything you want to show*
no stress, no worry   *and don't need to say sorry*
no apologies needed, no need to say sorry
all you know   *anything you want to show*
no stress, no worry   *and don't need to say sorry*
no apologies needed, no need to say sorry
all you want to have   *is there before you*
all you need to have   *is everything before you*
just remember the condition

no more talking snakes
no more talking snakes
no more burning tree
no more eating the fee

you can see the beauty in eve's garden
the mistake you make, long life and love sworn in
you may pledge to God in hope for forgiveness
its your garden and you can live in it or be left a burden
there's no mercy and no sign to cheat your way out of this
I can see your in pain, the beauty is within the garden
just don't abuse it with destructiveness
don't lose it because it belongs to us
I see you now there is no use, to refuse its attractiveness
enjoy it as you see it because its your garden

no more talking snakes
no more talking snakes
no more burning tree
no more eating the fee

as you believe do you deceive?
ask yourself do you know now
what you're getting yourself into
do you agree?

let's get ready
let's get ready
all you know   *anything you want to show*
no stress, no worry   *and don't need to say sorry*
no apologies needed, no need to say sorry
all you know   *anything you want to show*
no stress, no worry   *and don't need to say sorry*
no apologies needed, no need to say sorry
all you want to have   *is there before you*
all you need to have   *is everything before you*
just remember the condition

no more talking snakes
no more talking snakes
no more burning tree
no more eating the fee

Symphony For Sympathy

press the key
can you read and see?
the love that was lost
touch the keys and see as well
as well understand, can you see?
see the way I was ?
before and after the way I once was
I'm scared to say it
can you help me step forward?

because this symphony was for you
can you hear it in my voice?
and the sympathy was here for you
and you'll be crying with your choice

I loved you then and now, until forever
can't you see the sympathy?
as I push the energy forward
the love within the symphony

I'm all broken up inside
and I can't stand this feeling of hurt
because I will never see you again
and I'm hurt   *and I'll never see you ever again*
watching outside my window, I'm watching the rain
the rain drops fall and its like tears falling from above
not the best to hear the thunder *because I won't see you again*
it comes roaring like a lion from way above

because this symphony was for you
can you hear it in my voice?
and the sympathy was here for you
and you'll be crying with your choice
I loved you then and now until forever
can't you see the sympathy?
as I push the energy forward
the love within the symphony
can you remember the things you did?
the way you were held in my arm
all the way, you looked at me and said
things you would do and that you would not cause me harm
I wish you were here even though I remember what you did
you will hear the symphony of sympathy

Madness

I can't stop this feeling
the feeling that is in my heart
what I am, having my eyes roll up to the ceiling
hope nothing bad happens like a broken heart
to keep this relationship from falling apart
its like going down a wild river
going down the rapids, this destructive river

if there's no romance I'll get off this river
the emotional hell that keeps going and going

the madness is in me
I can't stop it
I want you so bad
I think you're so bad
so can't you see
I've been put in sudden rage

I cry when I can't have you
can you see the tears falling down
and I don't know what to do
these tears are for you and when they fall they carry sound
but I'll never give up, I don't know how to give up
until I have you, the world will be at my feet
all I want is you
as much as anything else to fulfill
and more than anyone would tell
I'm looking out for you and I'm on fire for you

the madness is in me	it makes me move faster
I can't stop it	it drives me crazy
I want you so bad	it makes me try harder
I think you're so bad	it sounds like thunder
so can't you see	the way you make me crazy

I'm put in a sudden rage and its because of you

I need you right now
I see you leave now, so proud
and it very quickly drives me mad
I'm alone in shame and you turn to watch me
then you walk away, without me
I can't see you anymore and you can't see me , there's nothing left to be
but I hope to see you tomorrow, more than clear
and you see me now and watch me draw near

the madness is in me	it makes me move faster

I can't stop it   it drives me crazy
I want you so bad   it makes me try harder
I think you're so bad   it sounds like thunder
so can't you see   the way you make me crazy
I'm put in a sudden rage and its because of you

The Fadedness

so here I am incomplete
having a few drinks and I'm all alone
sitting down having a seat
here I am on the phone
but I don't hear nothing from you
except for the tone
I'm looking for you
because after all, I need you

I'm in a fading blanking state
under the covers hiding from fate
can't understand you and your hate
I need you now, together forever
for I'd rather fade
than to be without you

I'm fading away while this takes place
it doesn't matter who I am color or race
she doesn't want me and I'm not going to worry
she's in love with another man and there's no haste
I don't care for this life
since I lost you
I have a feeling of being stabbed in the heart from your knife
its all I can prove, there's nothing left I can do
to be with you
my soul has disappeared within myself
the ratio for love has ended for me, I'm falling deeper within myself
I can't see the globe or beautiful light within myself
 going on and on to eternity and in the universe

I'm in a fading blanking state
under the covers hiding from fate
can't understand you and your hate
I need you now together
for I'd rather fade
than to be without you

Satan has taken over me
so you can't see me
and he won't let me be
the one and only one for me
do you want to leave me in darkness?

I'm in a fading blanking state
under the covers hiding from fate
can't understand you and your hate
I need you now, together forever
for I'd rather fade
than to be without you

The Attack Force

they say attack is the very last word
peace and struggle shall last
the future, the more you know of the past
they only see it right and see it once

there's nothing
nothing can stop them
there's something
nothing you can do to break them
they're many
the powerful mark for bravery
they're here
you know and help them
there's nothing here that can stop them

they know their powered
they know their coward
they know who to stop
they can help save the world
don't worry they'll hurry
they hear you all the way
super or not there here, in a hurry
because you'll never be wrong at all

there's nothing
nothing can stop them
there's something
nothing you can do to break them
they're many
the powerful mark for bravery
they're here
you know and help them
there's nothing here that can stop them

Deep Fur

I can only chase you so far
and I can only see you so far
I can hear you, but I can't see you
you're invisible to me
but I know you're near
and when I have you trapped
I'll wait for your fear
I stick my finger out for a tap
and I say

whatcha gonna do now
whatcha gonna do now
whatcha gonna do now
whatcha gonna do now

deep fur

I grab your legs and watch you struggle
and so you struggle
I hear you squeak and shriek
I can tell you're brave
and wait for the time
because time is for those who want to feel safe
and I say
where you were
where you are
would you hide?

whatcha gonna do now
whatcha gonna do now
whatcha gonna do now
whatcha gonna do now
deep fur

you wanna play games?
I'll be the jackal
you'll be the rabbit
tied in a knot
are you in a pickle?
we'll play day and night
and I'll make you tickle
redness and heat
down somewhere hot
and I say

whatcha gonna do now
whatcha gonna do now
whatcha gonna do now
whatcha gonna do now
deep fur

rising in fun
the hunt shall never end

all play and no end
you won't win
you see the others side
and yet you can't arrive
just enjoy the ride
and I say

whatcha gonna do now
whatcha gonna do now
whatcha gonna do now
whatcha gonna do now
deep fur

whatcha gonna do now
whatcha gonna do now
whatcha gonna do now
whatcha gonna do now
deep fur

I Don't Care

I don't care
who we are
I don't care what we wear
in a different place
on another star
with a sprinkled race
on the edge of forever

I don't care
where we go
in a place made of gold
we see in a sudden stare
I don't care
where it ends
where sunlight goes
and darkness ends
I don't care

would you care?
where you were
would you hide?
where you were?
do you care?
where you are
do you know?
where you are

deep above   high above
in the clouds   of love
where problems   are all ready to be solve
do you hear the little dove?
way up high, way up above

I don't care
where we go
in a place made of gold
we see in a sudden stare
I don't care
where it ends
where sunlight goes
and darkness ends
I don't care

free from us
away from us
turned to dust
a change to lust
a loss from us

do you care?
do you think its fair?
is it here
we don't need them
because who cares
what they say

because who cares
I don't

I don't care
where we go
on a place of gold
we see in a sudden stare
I don't care
where it ends
where sunlight goes
and darkness ends
I don't care

give me your hand
and we'll leave this empty land
to a far away place
far away place

do you care?
then come with me
because you don't need them
I don't need them
and they don't care
we don't care
and I don't care

we don't need them
keep the lights dim
because certain people are chosen
for the special occasion

I don't care
where we go
in a place made of gold
we see in a sudden stare
I don't care
where it ends
where sunlight goes

and darkness ends
I don't care

I don't care
where we go
in a place made of gold
we see in a sudden stare
I don't care
where it ends
where sunlight goes
and darkness ends
I don't care

<u>Ain't So Bad After All</u>

throughout the world
I see in our eyes, coexistence and acceptance
evolving around us
every single minute of the day
but why do we pay
by using up everything around us
destroying the rain forest for today
you can cry whenever you see this happen
and it happens all the time
and diseases comes out with a vengeance
striking us like wild fire like there's no compliance
just raise your head and look around the world
you will see the world fight back against us

down on goes, comes the rain
all the others of our kind don't speak the same
you can feel the rain hit your face to hide the pain
this world ain't so bad after all
we can heal the hurt when it came
we may find a way to live
for all living things and us will not be insane
we will find a way to live
feel the rain run down your face

and realize it ain't so bad after all

it ain't so bad after all
it ain't so bad after all
and it ain't so bad after all

there is something leaking, its a hole in the sky
the destructive sun and radiation, we will surely die
when will we ever realize
how we can kill ourselves with these lies
we may find a way to live
with this destruction in people's lives
we can survive
give us time to realize
what we see through our eyes

down on goes, comes the rain
all the others of our kind don't speak the same
you can feel the rain hit your face to hide the pain
this world ain't so bad after all
we can heal the hurt when it came
we may find a way to live
for all living things and us will not be insane
we will find a way to live
feel the rain run down your face
and realize it ain't so bad after all

it ain't so bad after all
it ain't so bad after all

and it ain't so bad after all
and it ain't so bad after all

Splintered Sliver

ends to know
where pain can grow
for sorrow I feel

this feels to real
from ends I show
for I will know
to never crow
I will never know

love can be like a sliver
and it never ending
it can deliver
the sadness of a heartbreak

its like a girl you like
she's someone you want
she's someone you cherish
and you want to love
but she doesn't care

she doesn't share
its never ending

the pain will be healed
day by day
the skin will be sealed
splintered sliver

the pain will be healed
day by day
the skin will be sealed
splintered sliver

I see my fantasy end and don't want what I get
I see the pain in my finger when I sit
its like the pain in my chest and its the pit
I can't disguise it and I can't fake it
its well within it
for where I sit I can only feel the pain
like the girl that broke my heart

the pain will be healed
day by day
the skin will be sealed
splintered sliver

the pain will be healed
day by day
the skin will be sealed
splintered sliver

Taking Control

I've been a young one at heart
I've been a fooled one at start
taking things and I have a lot of regrets
I'm made to feel its wrong for taking the stuff
this stuff called love
I feel a thin edge of a sword on my face I feel its rough
I've felt I could lose control
each day unend, I try to stay and keep my hold
I can stand up much higher and I feel like I'm against a real player
bigger problems offer me nothing, but more emptiness
what should I do?

I'm taking control
I refuse to take any more
taking control
the things you stole from me
I'm taking control
stay away from me

yes I know
I heard your demands
the persecutions to be myself and you know
I heard the demands
the accusations of what I'm guilty of and your intimidation
or is it discrimination?
I sense the violence from your eyes

and you think you can tell me what to do
I used to be scared of you
but I got through to you, now I'm laughing at you
I won't take anymore, anymore of you
you can't tell me what to do

I'm taking control
I refuse to take anymore
taking control
taking control
taking control
taking control

I'm taking control
I refuse to take any more
taking control
the things you stole from me
I'm taking control
stay away from me
the things you stole from me
I'm taking control
stay away from me

I'm taking control

you think you control my fears?
you think I'm scared, but I'll rise
I'll be on my feet and I'll come after you
I had nothing inside me, but now there's no good-byes
you used to know me and think I was weak,
but now I'll rise, I'll wipe my tears
I won't back down and I'll become wise
and now I know how to hurt you
I'll strike you down and take the deepest rout
with my kitchen knife I'll dig in your chest
I'll dig deep and take the road that leads to your heart
so can you see?
I'm taking your heart

and I won't stop
until you wish you left me alone

I'm taking control
I refuse to take any more
taking control
taking control
taking control
taking control

I'm taking control
I refuse to take any more
taking control
the things you stole from me
I'm taking control
stay away from me
the things you stole from me
I'm taking control
stay away from me

taking control
taking control
taking control
I'm taking control

Music In My Head

what a strange place of being
its the way you can see it
what a strange way of seeing
a place where you can sit
I can read I can write
can you see it, in front of your sight?

I've got this thing in my head
its as plain as it is said
whatever I see, whatever I read
is fed, in my head, with what I've read

Red Dragon Fantasy; Song Lyrics and Poetry

I said
I've got this thing in my head
its as plain as it is said
whatever I see whatever I've read
is fed in my head with what I've read
I tell you
I've got music in my head
I've got music in my head

you have a strange way of seeing it
a weird way of feeding it
where I come from
only the mind is working
the images are real
where I've been seeking
the things I have to deal

I've got this thing in my head
its as plain as it is said
whatever I see, whatever I read
is fed, in my head, with what I've read
I said
I've got this thing in my head
its as plain as it is said
whatever I see whatever I've read
is fed in my head with what I've read
I tell you
I've got music in my head
I've got music in my head

don't you believe me?
wont you tell me?
why?
say it to me
music that's in my head
tell me now
music in my head
music in my head

I've got this thing in my head
its as plain as it is said
whatever I see, whatever I read
is fed, in my head, with what I've read
I said
I've got this thing in my head
its as plain as it is said
whatever I see whatever I've read
is fed in my head with what I've read
I tell you
I've got music in my head
I've got music in my head

Brain Storming

things that we know of
things that we have heard of
things that we see of
things that we don't care of

I don't know where we are
but we are a star to far
I think we can go home right now
its been raining out for hours
and now its finally quit

how have you been doing?
I've just been brain storming
how have you been doing?
I've just been brain storming
how have you been doing?
I've just been brain storming

things that we can see
where everything we think of, is free
all is out, there all we can see
we're way up there

in a trance, in a stare
I can't believe how fare we are
how high we are

I don't know how far we are
but we are too far
I think we can go home right now
its been raining for hours and its finally quit

how have you been doing?
I've just been brain storming
how have you been doing?
I've just been brain storming
how have you been doing?
I've just been brain storming

there are things that we could tell
but there's nothing there to sell
the things that we can see
where everything we think of is for free
all is out and its all we can see

how have you been doing?
I've just been brain storming
how have you been doing?
I've just been brain storming
how have you been doing?
I've just been brain storming

Blue Soundra

oh stay way up high to the nice blue sky
to the blue nights soundra
from me to you
feel the beat in the sky
feel the music midnight sky
feel the party and you'll know why

Red Dragon Fantasy; Song Lyrics and Poetry

I feel the heat way up here
solemn to you and there's much to do
no need to worry
no need to fear
don't have to apologize or say sorry
just sit back and enjoy the party

blue soundra
is within us together
blue soundra
we'll be together forever
blue soundra

get the party
in the party
how's the party?
for everybody

way up high
in a place where everyone gets along
way above the sky
that's where it is where you hear t is strong
that blue soundra
has got me going
we'll never stop and we won't give up
way up high as high as the Luna
that's where it is
and that's where we're going
I can't wait until it starts
one more time, for hero's sake
way up high, way up high
that's where we belong

the soundra
is within us together
blue soundra
we'll be together
blue soundra

we'll party all night with no other

get the party
in the party
how's the party?
for everybody

blue soundra
is within us together
blue soundra
we'll be together forever
blue soundra

Language of Love

can you tell what I'm speaking
I'm speaking a different language
can you tell
I've been in trouble seeing and freeing
others of your kind
would you know what I'm speaking?
if I asked you

you might be smart
and your wealth at start
because this is my language
my love is my wisdom
and you might be too
I've been speaking the language of love
do you know?
what I've been saying?
and where I'll send you?

do you know?
what I've been saying?
when I send you
from me to you
can you reach me?

you're the one I want to see

you might be smart
and your wealth at start
because this is my language
my love is my wisdom
and you might be too
I've been speaking the language of love
do you know?
what I've been saying?
where I send you?

I can't explain to you
how much I want to be with you
I want to be with you

I can't describe to you
how much I want to be with you
I want to be with you

you might be smart
and your wealth at start
because this is my language
my love is my wisdom
and you might be too
I've been speaking the language of love
do you know?
what I've been saying?
and where I'll send you?

Dazed Vision Of Light In Fright

How Do I Escape This Nightmare?
Jump On Fire
Why Don't You Believe In Me?
I Am Am I?
Vision Union Reunion
Does It Really Matter? (original)
High Sky
Dominant People
Tandy
The Kiss Of The Widow
The Lonely Child
Dazed Vision
Blind Spot
Admission 3:55
Your Light In Fright
God Child
The Stuff Dreams Are Made Of
It Must Have Been
Then Leave Me Alone
The Legend Never Dies
Angels From Hell
Does It Really Matter? II

How Do I Escape This Nightmare?

I've fallen asleep
and I can't escape
I've been searching for you
I thought you were her
I can't see where I'm going
I'm stumbling in the dark and I can't hear
I'm losing myself in this dream, this scary dream
I'm camouflaged within this night and I want to end the fight
I suddenly hear screaming and it ends with laughing and then I feel fear

I'm locked in my dream
after I get used to sleeping twelve hours
I'm living a world that's black and white
and I don't want to leave
its a dream about me and my sisters and its not ours
its about people we don't like and there's no bright light
and I ask the question

how do I escape this nightmare?
in a place on a land
where no one cares and nothing is fair
how do I escape this nightmare?

how do I escape this nightmare?
am I in a school or a prison?
how do I escape this nightmare
am I in the USA or Thailand?
how do I escape this nightmare?

that's where I've been living
in my own world of sleeping
you can hear me breathing
in this world I'm dreaming
everyone lost their will to keep believing
but I haven't and I'll keep fighting

I'll find a way to escape this nightmare

the fear of failure fills me well inside my soul
the fear inside
there's no place to hide
how will I escape?
I can imagine the women in a rape
the demons can hear me and they're laughing at me
the fallens can see me and they're attacking me
the vultures are flying down on me
why am I running?
when I know they are coming for me
I can't escape
this insane rape
that they put me through
and there's nothing more that I can do

how do I escape this nightmare?
in a place, on a land
where no one cares and nothing is fair
how do I escape this nightmare?

how do I escape this nightmare?
am I in a school or a prison?
how do I escape this nightmare
am I in the USA or China?
how do I escape this nightmare?

I'm in complete darkness
will you tell me that they gone too far
I'm in complete darkness
tell me they gone too far
oh please   oh please
how do I escape this nightmare?
how do I escape the nightmare?
how do I escape this nightmare?

it ain't fair

no answers from my prayer
that I dare
how do I escape this nightmare?
                        this nightmare
                                this nightmare
                                            nightmare

how do I escape this nightmare?
in a place on a land
where no one cares and nothing is fair
how do I escape this nightmare?

how do I escape this nightmare?
am I in a school or a prison?
how do I escape this nightmare
am I in the USA or Soviet Union?
how do I escape this nightmare?

Jump On Fire

jump on
jump on fire
jump on
jump on fire
jump on
jump on fire

I can feel the heat
my hands got blisters
I can feel my chest flutter with each heartbeat
boys and girls are in the weight room, misses and misters

are you getting hot?
hot and sweaty
show me what your made of
within your power
you're all set and ready
you're taller and stronger

than your suppose to be
lift in shape lets watch and see

I'm in the weight room
and I see you look at me
I begin to smile when I know you like me
we could lift weights together
leave your boyfriend and stay with me forever
stay forever in the weight room
and feel our hearts start on fire

jump on
jump on fire
jump on
jump on fire
jump on
jump on fire

are you getting sopped?
muscular and strong
nice and tough
show me who you fought
within your soul you're in a place that judges

you're toned and topped
you're power and stronger
better than ever
better than your suppose to be
lift your arms in shape
you turn to look at me
and wonder how it would be
let's watch and see

I'm in the weight room
and I see you look at me
I begin to smile when I know you like me
we could lift weights together
leave your boyfriend and stay with me forever

stay forever in the weight room
and feel our hearts start on fire

jump on
jump on fire
jump on
jump on fire
jump on
jump on fire

your stronger than your suppose to be
all you see not much more you can be
the jump has ended just as the heat
blisters and sours at the end of your hands and feet

jump on
jump on fire
jump on
jump on fire
jump on
jump on fire

Why Don't You Believe In Me?

there it was drifting
within my mind
turning and shifting
where it was I find
feeling alone
feeling alone
feeling alone

always alone
I talk on the phone
where I live
in my home

let it soar

let it fly
more and more
high as high
make the image explode so high

in my world I'm a king and I make believe that I can fly
in my world my sister helped create a world that will never die
in this world nobody can enter because they don't believe us
I bring this world out in animation and illustration into my reality
the humanoids don't believe me and they don't care
they sit and laugh hysterically and make us cry in anger
and I ask why?

why?
why don't you believe in me?
stay with me and see
why?
why don't you believe in me?
I'm creating my world in this reality
I feel so hurt, your words of hurt
can you see it?

why?
why don't you believe in us?
stay with me and watch us
why?
why don't you believe in us?
we're creating our world in this reality
I feel so hurt, your words of hurt
can you see it?

home stock summers
the greatest place to be
away from harm and free
great sun summers
things to do, things to see
I pull out my pencil

and start to write and illustrate

I can already hear my parents tell me
snap into reality and start your life
like everyone else your under competition
throw away these childish dreams, do you get me?
you will graduate high school and go to college to be

why do you knock me back?
I'm taken back
I don't know what to say
the hurt within me
it hurts to see me
when its something negative you say

let it soar
let it fly
more and more
high as high
make the image explode so high

in my world I'm a king and my sister is a queen and we make believe that we can fly
in this world my sister helped create a world that will never die and we'll never die
in this world nobody can enter because they don't believe us
I bring this world out in animation and illustration to my reality
my sister breathes life to this world and says who will live and who will die
the sub-humans don't believe me and they don't care about our real fantasy
they laugh hysterically and make us really pissed off in anger
and I demand to know why?

why?
why don't you believe in me?
stay with me and see
why?

why don't you believe in me?
I'm creating my world in this reality
I feel so hurt   your words of hurt
can you see it?

why?
why don't you believe in us?
stay with me and watch us
why?
why don't you believe in us?
we're creating our world in this reality
I feel so hurt, your words of hurt
can you see it?
I can feel your hurt
can you see it?

I Am, Am I?

I am what I am, where I am,
am I?
nothing, no one can change me for what I am why I am,
am I?
I am what I am, how I am,
am I?

no one here can change me for who I am,
am I?
I can change what I am, where I am , why I am,
am I?

but I won't
because I am what I am,
am I?
no one can change me more than what I am
who I am, where I am,
am I?
and I am, who I am, where I am, when I am,
am I?

no one can change me more than who I am
who I am, where I am,
am I?

my heart is what I am how I am
my heart is why I am now I am, am I?
I am what I am, am I?
no one no how can change my heart of what I am who I am, am I?
do you like me for who I am?
of what I am?
where I am,
am I?
do you want me to change?
do you want me to change for you? to be like them?
expectation I feel from you to me
I would rather die than to be like everyone else

and I won't
because I am what I am,
am I?
no one can change me more than what I am
who I am, where I am,
am I?
and I am, who I am, where I am, when I am,
am I?
no one can change me more than who I am
who I am, where I am,
am I?

I am
I am
I am
I am

am I?

Vision Union Reunion

I see the future
of us together again
seeing the future
of us not in pain
I see a vision
where we make a decision
life or death?
where it is for the future to begin

counter break time
reunite us
fowlers play time
can't you see

you can live in a vision union reunion
you can feel free in a vision union reunion
an imagination of a vision union reunion
a vision union reunion

together, together as one
put us together
when everyone joins our USA flag
and we live without another plague
pull us together away from the other
as peace as we know
which now shall go
I see a dream
to unite us as it would seem
I can see the future where everyone will want to be like us
that's where it lies
in a world of freedom and no one dies

counter break time
reunite us
fowlers play time
can't you see

you can live in a vision union reunion
you can feel free in a vision union reunion
an imagination of a vision union reunion
a vision union reunion

Does It Really Matter? (Original)

would you really know me
if I came up to you, to say hi
last words through our eyes
I say to you goodbye
has it been this long
that you can't remember me
would it really matter
if you wanted to see me again
since your taken
I feel alone
feeling mistaken
would you know?

would it really matter to you?
if I came over to meet you
I know it has been so long
too long to be apart
first contact, to first thought, not much can be said to you
since you're not alone

don't have to say much for words
I can see it in your eyes
how much you remembered me
same as done for me
because look at how long it has been
since I saw you
many times I wondered
does it really matter?
that I've seen you
do you think about me? as would I

would you want to see me?
since you're not alone
would it even matter to change your mind?
of the way I felt about you

would it really matter to you?
if I came over to meet you
I know it has been so long
too long to be apart
first contact to first thought not much can be said to you
since you're not alone

I know your happy to see me as well as I am for you
I had always wondered about you
throughout the end of time
I have always wanted to see you
but I had been afraid
does it really matter?
now, since you're not alone

High Sky

free at last
ready to go home
not wasting much time
because I'm not grounded
and found where I don't belong
flying high
speeding fast
as fast as I can

flying like superman
higher and higher
faster than a rocket
moving lighter and lighter
its like my arm being pulled from its socket

high sky

the things they say can make me
high sky
away from this hiding so they can see
high sky
I startle myself and yell out in a cry
high sky
where I'm free at last and I'll know why
I say high sky

free at last
away from the past
away from the disgust
ready to get away
out from the negative people today
flying high and away so I can trust

high sky
the things they say can make me
high sky
away from this hiding so they can see
high sky
I startle myself and yell out in a cry
high sky
where I'm free at last and I'll know why
I say high sky

Dominant People

man as they say will master themselves
take a stand do you master yourself?
people as they say are masters of themselves
and they will only listen to themselves

in this world there are people who will lead themselves
they don't need anyone telling them what to do
no class mate, no neighbor, no teacher, no priest
telling them what to do or how to live their life

you can live in this world and lead yourself
you won't need anyone telling you what to do
no bullies, jocks, teachers, principals, social workers
telling you what to do or how to live your life

dominononouse
cower before me
dominononouse
lower than before me
dominononouse
others free to be higher than me
just the way
its supposed to be in the USA

dominononouse
dominant people
dominononouse
dominant people
dominononouse
dominant people

these people are masters of themselves
they'll be the new leaders of themselves
these mighty rulers will decide for themselves
too many fake leaders sitting in cushy chairs
too many fake politics sitting in cushy chairs
they destroy our dreams and break our hearts
from these higher levels they will collapse
defenses seem negative, but they will kill themselves
and in will come the survivors, the dominant people
the self-leaders, dominononouse

dominononouse
cower before me
dominononouse
lower than before me
dominononouse
others free to be higher than me

just the way
its supposed to be in the USA

dominononouse
dominant people
dominononouse
dominant people
dominononouse
dominant people

domminononouse,
dominononouse people
dominononouse
striking each other
dominononouse
hurting each other
dominononouse,

the hate streak and we'll attack each other
affecting one from another
chorus of love for our sister and brother
extinguish the authorities who want to control the other
purpose for us to rule ourselves not each other

dominononouse
cower before me
dominononouse
lower than before me
dominononouse
others free to be higher than me
just the way
its supposed to be in the USA

dominononouse
dominant people
dominononouse
dominant people
dominononouse

dominant people

Tandy

oh Tandy
you're so sweet
sweet as candy
you were as sweet as can be
oh Tandy you know I loved to be with you
Tandy you know it can't be easy
but you know I can take it easy

you were the girl I wanted to love
the woman of my dreams, the white dove
I held you at a high steed, I watched you dance
In my sister's dance class, you were so beautiful
so wonderful and I wanted to give you a chance

oh Tandy you were feeling your out of place
you need your own little space
I saw it on your face
the pain that hurts with your poor face

you were feeling out of place when you tore my heart from beneath my chest
I got your autograph when you were a star
and I got you phone number and called you up
to get my heart ripped from my chest

oh Tandy you know you can come to me
you'll survive with me and be with me
I know it must hurt being so far away
look at me tell me what is wrong you
know you can tell me what's wrong
and I know what's wrong when you led me on

oh Tandy *you're not*
candy

please don't hurt me now
I suppose through all you've been through
you never knew what it was like
laughing and being as free
free in mind on bike
I'll be understanding
when you mean you won't be coming home at all

*you ripped my
heart apart
and everything
I've been through
to be the man
on the other end
laughing at me
and you'll
know what its like
to be the bitch
under my foot
and that you're
a whore*

oh Tandy
you're not sweet as candy
you're a whore in the making
you were once as sweet as can be
but you'll end up with some loser with ten kids from ten different dads
oh Tandy I wish you were here with me, but I know its a fantasy

The Kiss Of The Widow

in the deep dark forest
you see before you
a face so scary
is she a woman?
and you don't know what to do

way up high in the trees with shadows of blue
I see before me
a face so pretty I don't know what to do
she manipulated me with her desires to see

this supernatural creature can hide her true form
she's the temptress that walks the night
she's the lioness that stalks her prey in dreams
you're the lamb and she'll kill you without a fight

she'll make you believe you'll live a life of porn
you'll nod your head to smile even though nothing is what it seems
until you get the kiss of the widow

why don't you come around
come so sweet
come around and kiss me
done so mean

you're the woman of my dreams
when nothing is what it seems
you can make love to me all night
and leave your spider bite on my neck
its like a million black widows crawling on me
and that is the way it should be
infect me with your poison
and make my life a living wreck
we can be married every night
because you're the girl of my dreams

so dazed to me, in my dazed vision
I can't tell by your bite, if you really love me
the need to carry on with you, haunts me every night
I am frightened by you, but I need you
but yet I'm confused by you, I need to make love with you
spun around in your web, your web of lies and deceit
I love this performance of illusion that are in my dreams
I'm caught in your web of defeats and I would love to be in your dreams
she waits to be my love catcher and its not what its seems
but I don't care because when I fall asleep I'll be her lover
spun around in these web of lies you'll wait your turn
its a dazed vision in dizziness and I still can't tell who you are
but I'll wait for the kiss of the widow

why don't you come around
come so sweet
come around and kiss me

Red Dragon Fantasy; Song Lyrics and Poetry

done so mean

you're the woman of my dreams
when nothing is what it seems
you can make love to me all night
and leave your spider bite on my neck
its like a million black widows crawling on me
and that is the way it should be
infect me with your poison
and make my life a living wreck
we can be married every night
because you're the girl of my dreams

kiss me
hug me
love me
like me

sacrifice me
with your stinger
stab in the heart
and when you pull the blade out
lick my blood with your forked tongue
and then

I'm scared to speak
I can hear my heart beat flip like a coin
I'm trying to keep clear
of the very right ones not to fear
where I say the last words and join
I linger for the kiss of the widow

why don't you come around
come so sweet
come around and kiss me
done so mean

you're the woman of my dreams
when nothing is what it seems
you can make love to me all night
and leave your spider bite on my neck
its like a million black widows crawling on me
and that is the way it should be
infect me with your poison
and make my life a living wreck
we can be married every night
because you're the girl of my dreams

Lonely Child

do you want to hear a long sad story?
born with a red heart, created with fury
my love has been broken into pieces
had to give up hope and I can't tell you why, why?
because of the sharp, destructive criticisms that has been said to me
as the lonely child

the lonely child, the only child
that's what I am, for now until this place dies
the lonely child
left behind and I'm too undecided
the lonely child
that's what I am, for now until peace dies

where I sob
in my deep heart and lonely heart
I get a cold feeling surrounding me, its all for myself
I don't want to tell myself
how much I miss myself, my old self
the way things used to be in the beginning
I need to think of things now and begin my brand new start
to make things go right
I need to end the loneliness
so end the long cold silence
of the lonely child

the lonely child, the only child
that's what I am, for now until this place dies
the lonely child
left behind and I'm too undecided
the lonely child
that's what I am, for now until peace dies

can you tell what I've been feeling?
I don't know where I've been
I hope the pain will be healing
things I ask to do and what I can
stand against my hope for a chance
the loneliness exhausts me
and they steal more pieces of my soul away
there's nothing that I can do and there's nothing I can say
my body is falling apart the way a car is left to rust and fall apart
as a lonely child, the only child

the lonely child, the only child
that's what I am, for now until this place dies
the lonely child
left behind and I'm too undecided
the lonely child
that's what I am, for now until peace dies

you too, discourage my luck
miss-understood in my life to my hope
you know its true
what you say suck
within my loneliness I see myself
and I really think I am my own friend
I don't rely on you
I say to myself
things you say, aren't they sin?
to what extent
they want to make me the lonely child
the only child

the lonely child, the only child
that's what I am, for now until this place dies
the lonely child
left behind and I'm too undecided
the lonely child
that's what I am, for now until peace dies

<u>My Dazed Vision</u>

the vision in my brain won't let you go
because I just wanted to let you know
how much I wanted to be with you
like so
the sight of you it makes me desire you
makes me want to be with you, it drives me to love you

I could still see your smile and makes me happy
your blonde hair, your brown eyes keeps me locked to you
when I watch you at your ballet it makes me cry
when I see how good you really are and it makes you happy
I see your power and it hypnotizes me, it makes me want to die
and my sister knows that I would do anything for you

why didn't you tell me?
how you felt toward me
why didn't you tell me?
that you didn't want to be seen by me
why didn't you tell me?
of how much you disliked me
why didn't you tell me?
of my dazed vision

its a dazed vision I live in
a dazed vision
like the vision in my brain
a dazed vision
the tears fall from my eyes and down the drain

a dazed vision
when you lead me on and treat me like I'm plain
a dazed vision
I can feel your dagger stab me, like its sin
A dazed vision

I see your emotions towards me
I tell my sister how much you mean to me
I relive the memories of when we first met, a fantasy in notion
I feel so alive, I feel so happy I feel immortal and its a fantasy set in motion
I rose for you, I treated you like a queen,
I got your autograph because you're a star and I made every excuse to see you
just to be with you
and then you led me on
why didn't you tell me?
how you felt toward me
why didn't you tell me?
that you didn't want to be seen by me
why didn't you tell me?
of how much you disliked me
why didn't you tell me?
of my dazed vision

its a dazed vision I live in
a dazed vision
like the vision in my brain
a dazed vision
the tears fall from my eyes and down the drain
a dazed vision
when you lead me on and treat me like I'm plain
a dazed vision
I can feel your dagger stab me like its sin
a dazed vision

can you see my soul?
can you remember my visits?

into your dreams
can't you see
I needed you
needed to be you
just to be with you

you were precious to me, innocent and beautiful
I can't use my vision
I would rather sew my eyes shut than to open my eyes
I hoped I was wrong and pray you'll talk to me
even after you hurt me, but I know you won't
because lead me on and said you have a boyfriend
even though I don't think you do

I wanted these moments to be
I wanted to be with you
just to see you
and through this dazed vision
I make believe I'm still with you   even though I should've been
just to be with you

why didn't you tell me?
how you felt toward me
why didn't you tell me?
that you didn't want to be seen by me
why didn't you tell me?
of how much you disliked me
why didn't you tell me?
of my dazed vision

its a dazed vision I live in
a dazed vision
like the vision in my brain
a dazed vision
the tears fall from my eyes and down the drain
a dazed vision
when you lead me on and treat me like I'm plain
a dazed vision

I can feel your dagger stab me like its sin
a dazed vision

Blind Spot

can you be stopping
stopping the problem
can you be helping stop the problem?
yeah!

you can say I have a problem
a problem with you and bullies in this school
in a small town with you   and I'm under the rule
and there's nothing else I can do

can you stop the pressure against me?   can you stop the pressure on me?
can you stop impressing me?   the downward spiral on me
just stop the pressure against me   and stop pressuring me
can you stop the pressure against me?   where I get persecuted for being me

my heart is open
whenever you want to look into it
in this school of dog eat dog
you can breed a chest full of maggots
whenever I am alone, I begin to miss my home
I can't stand the message from them
that I keep receiving to give up your dreams
its like a blind spot
the blind spot begins to grow
it grows and grows
older and older
and I feel that I am
wiser and wiser
but as I fail I feel the blind spot grows
wider and wider until it eats me whole

can you stop the pressure against me?   can you stop the pressure on me?
can you stop impressing me?   the downward spiral on me
just stop the pressure against me   and stop pressuring me
can you stop the pressure against me?   where I get persecuted for being me

black and small that's how they make me feel
nothing to do except pretend I'm doing well
I feel like I'm possessed by the devil as I have nothing to feel
the dark shadows of soulless humanoids don't want me well
I look around to see what it is before me
the problem of tomorrow and I hope I'll be able to see

these soulless sub-humans will do anything to bring you down
you can tell them your wildest dreams and they'll go and tell
they'll tell you no and make you believe it
they'll tell you where to go and force you to see it

can you stop the pressure against me?   can you stop the pressure on me?
can you stop impressing me?   the downward spiral on me
just stop the pressure against me   and stop pressuring me
can you stop the pressure against me?   where I get persecuted for being me

my heart is open
whenever you want to look into it
in this school of dog eat dog
you can breed a chest full of maggots
whenever I am alone, I begin to miss my home
I can't stand the message from them
that I keep receiving to give up your dreams
its like a blind spot
the blind spot begins to grow
it grows and grows
older and older
and I feel that I am

wiser and wiser
but as I fail I feel the blind spot grows
wider and wider until it eats me whole

can you stop the pressure against me?   can you stop the pressure on me?
can you stop impressing me?   the downward spiral on me
just stop the pressure against me   and stop pressuring me
can you stop the pressure against me?   where I get persecuted for being me

Admission 3:55

you were the one
that I liked very much, the one I wanted very much
the one that I felt strongly towards
I left everything behind in my little town
to go, come down and visit, to be with you

I see your beautiful long black hair
and your hypnotic blue eyes
it was so wonderful to see you here
I see you smile and everything seems fair
but like every relationship it ends in sad good-byes
we get a photo and I can tell you don't care
and I know I'm not the only one here, I'm not the only competing for you love
life is too short to get upset and life isn't always fair

year after year
I've been waiting here for you
year after year
I've been waiting here for you
year after year
I'll be waiting here for you

admission 3:55
I'll be taking the bus to visit you

admission 3:55
I'll be thinking about you
admission 3:55
I'll be dreaming about you
admission 3:55
a reality of friendship for you
admission 3:55

after I look at my ticket
I sit to wait for you
I look at my watch and its almost time
is it time to go? everyone is leaving to go home
I fear I made a mistake, but then I see you come
I'm blown away at how attractive you are

day after day, we make each day
and I can tell I'm not the one you want

every word cuts like a knife and its more than I can say
you could be more than my pen pal, you could be my best friend
and we could make it more than you could ever want
but its not what you want and all I am is a friend

year after year
I've been waiting here for you
year after year
I've been waiting here for you
year after year
I'll be waiting here for you

admission 3:55
I'll be taking the bus to visit you
admission 3:55
I'll be thinking about you
admission 3:55
I'll be dreaming about you
admission 3:55
a reality of friendship for you

admission 3:55

I got a round class ticket
got a long cost ride before me
can't stand the wait
the common mark hysteric state

I roll the window down
to get some last words to you
the first few days with you
were a blessing
I said that the last few words to you and they were meant for you

I saved the last few words and they were meant for you

year after year
I've been waiting here for you
year after year
I've been waiting here for you
year after year
I'll be waiting here for you

admission 3:55
I'll be taking the bus to visit you
admission 3:55
I'll be thinking about you
admission 3:55
I'll be dreaming about you
admission 3:55
a reality of friendship for you
admission 3:55

Your Light In Fright

can you close your eyes?
can you tell me your name?
relationships start with a hello and end with goodbyes
you feel upset, but you try to get attention by going out for fame

your falling apart and you try to keep it together, but you find out its not the same
because

when lightning strikes it leaves you burning
it gives you flashes in your eyes
and you'll remember what you have gone through
its a flash that ignites the moment and makes it so
and when your moment breaks you'll know they were lies
your eyes will be wide open and you won't believe it
but you'll know its happening and you'll have to make a stand
otherwise your light in fright won't survive

your strong hold caves in and shatters your dreams
and you'll realize that all there was, was not what seems
its an illusion a powerful illusion that binds you in the darkness
its all fake, a Trojan horse to keep you in blindness

when lightning strikes it leaves you screaming
it unleashes the tears from your eyes
and you'll be left thinking about her eyes,
when you go after the girl of your dreams
its a flash that explodes the fantasy that wakes you up to what it seems
and when your reality bursts you'll know she told you lies
your ears will be ringing and your eyes will be immersed in tears
you don't believe it, you won't believe it, but you'll realize its the truth
and you'll know its happening and you'll have to make a stand
otherwise your light in fright won't survive

I want you to close your hands
put them into mine
I'm your higher self, your true friend
your new but old
and you're out on your own

I can tell you you're weathered like a piece of paper
a piece of paper that is taped with rips and folds
can you see the words that tell you to make a new start

the truth is untold but your future is revealed
the future is torn, but it can be healed
she trapped you like gold to eat you whole
can you feel your whole? look at the sky and begin to rectify

God Child

I'm just sitting, waiting here, for hope to clear
for my time to come, only compared to some
I'm just waiting here for life to take its place
I am a thousand years old and I feel I'm the only one
if I am immortal I could be, I could see, and take my place

the fear that I must take drives me crazy
the sudden loss from my mistake causes me to tear
you think you can break me? break me? break me?
fake me? fake me? fake me? fake me?

god child
take all you want
god child
spoiled rotten, that you are
god child
we'll see how far you are
god child
and how far you get

Christmas presents and birthday toys
all that you want and everything you want
I don't have to love you
but I have to live with you
frostings and cupcakes, there all for you
your no longer a Jehovah Witness
and you've been starved for so long
you can imagine its all for you

you can have it all, watch rated "R" movies
listen to death metal and watch porno star movies

you don't have to worry about what other children have
just mind what you have and what you're going to have
do not cry, don't scream or shout and don't even think to mis-behave

you can have it all, listen to the radio of foul language
listen to others with respect and learn a foreign language
understand people for who they are and not their religion
stuff yourself with love, friendships and lovers get yourself fat and free of religion
get the things you want, push for the things you think about,
strive for the things in your mind
all you have to do is grab it
and you will have it

the fear that I must take drives me crazy
the sudden loss from my mistake causes me to tear
you think you can break me? break me? break me?
fake me? fake me? fake me? fake me?

god child
take all you want
god child
spoiled rotten, that you are
god child
we'll see how far you are
god child
and how far you get

you think you can break me? break me? break me?
fake me? fake me? fake me? fake me?

The Stuff Dreams Are Made Of

I circle around in the midnight sky
waiting for you to see me
I got a recipe for what you want
want and need, you want to know why?

the possessions you feed
can you show me what you're made of
made so sweet and when we meet
I can tell you what you can solve

I'll show you a dream that we can live in
the stuff where dreams are made of
a place of well being
playing with other that will hear us singing
the stuff that dreams are made of

It Must Have Been

it felt good
to see you again
from the moment we touched
until the moment you left
you were like a ghost
and I was left alone
to face the world

I'll give you these golden letters that will turn into fire
I'll hear you whisper in my ear and it drives my desire
you whisper my name and I know you came
I see you gesture with a smile
I see these golden letters sit in a pile
they look the same
it must have been good to throw these letters in the sky
they started on fire and it was like the first time
 we saw each other's own eyes and I thought I was going to die

these letters that came are beyond any ancient treasures
these letter are made of fire and gold, they give us pleasures
they fit together like a puzzle and say how much I love you
and they make me smile because it must have been you

it must have been you
please take my hand
it must have been you
the power of love that comes with silence
it must have been you
the ghost from a hidden land
it must have been you
that hears my whispers in dreams and can move the sand
it must have been you
that spells out the words I love you in letter made of gold and fire
it must have been you
for your heart I would walk through fire and die in a war
it must have been you

I loved you once
before and after we touched
can you handle my destiny
because along will come the silence of death
memories we hold are sad while others may be wonderful and funny

use the magic and use the power
animate these golden letters made of fire
make them return in your hands
you've done well to spell out your love of desire
now you must move on and let me take the steps
and let me think about how it must have been
I'll take the letters and re-ignite them in the sky
to show my love for you and you'll know why

it must have been you
please take my hand
it must have been you

the power of love that comes with silence
it must have been you
the ghost from a hidden land
it must have been you
that hears my whispers in dreams and can move the sand
it must have been you
that spells out the words I love you in letter made of gold and fire
it must have been you
for your heart I would walk through fire and die in a war
it must have been you

Then Leave Me Alone

all through the years
I felt the power of an adrenaline rush
it runs in my arms and through my legs
I feel even stronger that I'm supposed to be
when I get out of my desk I see how scared you are
when you look at me
I can't explain it and I won't deny it
I feel satisfaction from it and a little bit of fear

I can hear the announcement of my call
when I walk down the halls
they back away from me, they stay away from me
I think its an understanding from me
a fear from the leaches of this school, a feeling from you
but I can't get it through to you
not then and not now, its like talking to the wall
until its too late, I still remember what you said

cool down
sit down
and I say
then leave me alone
then leave me alone
leave me alone
    leave me alone

Red Dragon Fantasy; Song Lyrics and Poetry

leave me alone

I'll stop, I'll stop
right now, right now
for now
and I say
then leave me alone
then leave me alone
leave me alone
      leave me alone
           leave me alone

it was planned out hate
you know I didn't want it
planed out fate
you know you deserved it
but when a boy can't deny it
and you have to say it
then say it
its like a moment after a big fight
in second grade for something that isn't right
we get sent to the principal's office
but I take the first bite
I say how it is, I'll shout and scream
and I'll say how fucked up this is
and how I told the teachers before it happened
nobody believed it and acted like it was a dream
and I'll say it again, how fucked up this school is
if you have to say it
then say it
and leave me the fuck alone!

cool down
sit down
and I say
then leave me alone
then leave me alone
leave me alone

Red Dragon Fantasy; Song Lyrics and Poetry

      leave me alone
             leave me alone

I'll stop, I'll stop
right now, right now
for now
and I say
then leave me alone
then leave me alone
leave me alone
      leave me alone
           leave me alone

if you want to call it a truce and call it freedom
as blue as the sky, as yellow as the sun
you can hope all you wanted to have won
while dazed my vision my vision is set
and since you like to spread rumors of me as the bad guy
and the kids at school are stupid enough to believe all the rumors
they'll believe everything they hear and think its real
can you imagine a man burning you alive in your house?
each bully in every school deserves to be burned alive
I'll buy you the matches and gasoline and say its about time
and you'll hear me say
leave me alone!

then leave me alone
      then leave me alone
           then leave me alone
                then leave me alone

I'm a coiled up cobra ready to snap
the same cobra coiled on the flag of our nation
the same person who's sick of being teased and bullied
I'm unleashed from your tauntings and gripped to your heart
I'll kill you with my venom before you can even start
and I'll hear you say

cool down   *you cool down*
sit down   *you sit down*
and I say
then leave me alone   *leave me alone*
then leave me alone   *leave me alone*
leave me alone
    leave me alone
        leave me alone

I'll stop, I'll stop   *you won't stop*
right now, right now   *until I beat the fuck out of you*
for now   *you'll be black and blue*
and I say   *you're other friends deserve the same*
as you
then leave me alone   *leave me alone*
then leave me alone   *leave me alone*
leave me alone
    leave me alone
        leave me alone

The Legend Never Dies

you won't die
I won't die
people have heard
people have served

the younger generations have decided to split
right from the map of living existence
the bad guy wins and sends you away in a hit
a good guy is gone, a good song is gone, for instance
the disappearance of one will later become many
its like a civilization to a metropolis from a town to a city
you realize that someone has lied
but you see the legend never dies

the legend never dies
you'll see the good guy rise

ancestors from a generation ago, which dies
but not the stories
people die every day and leave pieces of them
do you wish you had something to send them?

wonder all around to see where you sit
playing musical chairs and find where you disappear
few guys win and send you away to reappear
lost out of existence you latter become many

civilization to metropolis from town to city
where you find people had said some lies
but you later find the legend never dies

the legend never dies
you'll see the good guy rise
ancestors from a generation ago, which dies
but not the stories
people die every day and leave behind pieces of them
do you wish you had something to send them?

Angels From Hell

they say they only come once
they wear disguises to hide
they steal the rides
they'll only come once
to steal your life

they are evil spirits that hate you
they look like they're your friend
they'll look at you with deceitful eyes
once they have what they want, there's nothing you can do
you can scream, you can run, do all you can
they're angels from hell

they are
angels from hell

insanity
demons from hell
vanity
fallens from hell
fantasy
angels from hell

angels from hell
demons that sell
fallens that rebel
dark entities that you can't tell

their wings spread far apart
they grind their teeth
they tear at your heart
while they stand on a reef
they'll creep out to you
they'll seep out to you
they wait for you
before they take over you

they are
angels from hell   *angels from hell*
insanity
demons from hell   *demons from hell*
vanity
fallens from hell   *fallens from hell*
fantasy
angels from hell

angels from hell
demons that sell
fallens that rebel
dark entities that you can't tell
they are angels from hell

they like to play games with the Ouija board
its so frustrating it happens when you're bored

can you sleep? can't you hide from this?
the only way to fight is in love, chants and the holy
and when you're finally through it, you'll know why
don't cry when you see them or try to defy
they're angels from hell

they are
angels from hell   *angels from hell*
insanity
demons from hell   *demons from hell*
vanity
fallens from hell   *fallens from hell*
fantasy
angels from hell
angels from hell
demons that sell
fallens that rebel
dark entities that you can't tell
they are angels from hell

they are angels from hell
they are angels from hell
they are angels from hell

they are angels from hell
they are angels from hell
they are angels from hell

Does It Really Matter? II

we find in this world what we don't expect
from the good and the bad
and throughout time I thought about you.

would you really know me?
if I came to you to say hello
last words through your eyes
in tears to you good-byes

does it really matter?

would it really matter?
if I came over to you
just to be with you
does it really matter?
that I've come over to meet you
to be one with you

does it really matter?
now, since you're not alone

I'm feeling pain
would you know?
don't say much for words
I can see it in your eyes
the way the memory has changed for you and I

has it been this long,
since this time
that you can't remember me?
would you want to see me?
since you're not alone
would it really matter?

would it really matter?
if I came over to you
just to be with you
does it really matter?
that I've come over to meet you
to be one with you

does it really matter?
now since you're not alone

would it really matter
if I came over to you
just to be with you   when I'm afraid of you

does it really matter that I've come over to meet you
to be one with you   when I dream of you

does it really matter, now
since you're not alone

Production Notes:

Production on the song lyrics had begun after 2011 when "What I Think About You: Song Lyrics and Poetry was published. The song lyrics were re-edited and re-structured to match up to the appropriate style of the song lyrics from What I Think About You: Song lyrics and Poetry. The original style was inferior and were written in phrases and incoherent thoughts that were not like the current 'mini story' song lyrics and poems. The song lyrics such as "Heart of Hell" and "Punishment From the Scarecrow" were re-edited to have the same dark tone as song lyrics like "Driving Nails Down Your Spine" and "Souls Under the Floor". The Poem"You're the Secret" was edited and a second version was written as a song lyric.

The song lyrics are divided into six sub-sections that range from heavy and heartless to sad and loving. They extend through the years of 1992 to the fall of 1994 and Spring of 1995. The sub-sections were "Heart of Hell", "Join or Die" , "This Magical Place", "Thunder Road Forever" and "Dazed Vision of Light and Fright".

Having sub-sections was important because each category was separate from the other and couldn't be mixed together. The song lyrics were also written to have first and second versus just as song lyrics do. Some song lyrics were written to rhyme using the AA BB format or the ABAB format and sometimes AAAA and BBBB format that was learned from English Class, Creative Writing and Advance English Class in high school.

Editing the song lyrics was difficult because Johnson didn't want to take away the originality of what he was trying to express in the compositions. His writing had matured since the 1990s and it was risky to make changes. The song lyrics also had some versus that rhymed that increased the difficulty to edit and change the song lyric for fear of changing the meaning or format of the song lyric. Very little changes were made to the "Thunder Road Forever" sub-section due to it's light song lyrics and poems.

The song lyrics after 1994 and 1995 to 1998 were cut to make a new collection of compositions for "Red Dragon Fantasy II: Song Lyrics and Poetry"

Red Dragon Fantasy: Song Lyrics and Poetry is a collection of song lyrics and poems written by the author Ryan Keith Johnson from 1991 to 1994 and 1995. The book is split up into six categories of dark, light, sad and love poems that reflected the author's feelings towards the event of the time.

About the Author:

Ryan Keith Johnson grew up in Somerset WI. He got into writing song lyrics and poems in 1991 and 1992. He was inspired to writing compositions because of his father. His first song lyric was "Killer Trolls" and then an earlier draft of "Heart of Hell". The author was in uncharted waters when writing these new compositions. They were structured in phrases and emotion versus logic and story telling, like many of the new ones are now.

The author continued to write song lyrics from 1992 all they way up to 1998, when he attended WITC. The "Slave Dancer" sub-section was eventually going to be a group of song lyrics that were going to be about one of his novels that was 850 pages handwritten. It was going to be something similar to a soundtrack for a movie, only this was going to pertain to one of his books. The project fell through when the author realized that the novel wasn't going to be published and the Slave Dancer sub-section was split up into three categories via "Slave Dancer I", "Slave Dancer II" and "Slave Dancer III" which ended up being published in "What I Think About You: Song Lyrics and Poetry.

After Going to college in Rice Lake, the author attended Brown Institute for graphic design and continued to write song lyrics from 2000-2010. He stopped writing song lyrics to publish "What I Think About You: Song Lyrics and Poetry". The song lyrics he wrote were mature and a little more complicated in their set up of having two sets of chorus or two sets of versus and followed the ABAB, BABA, AAAA or BBBB format and also had intro chorus before the main chorus. The song lyrics in the 90s had a simple set up of an ABAB format which meant the words would rhyme with each other and were rudimentry.

Following the publishing of "What I Think About You: Song Lyrics and Poetry. Johnson published "The Legacy Anthology" in 2012. Editing of the song lyrics commenced in 2009 to give the song lyrics and updated appeal vs the eighth grade immaturity of the earlier work. Editing the song lyrics was time consuming and not all the compositions needed editing. Some of them only needed re-arrangements and spelling. Due to the nature of a head on collision in 2006, Johnson decided that he wanted to put the entire collection in a book so that nothing would be lost. The car accident shook him up and made him fear for his life. He pushed forward to have the collection of song lyrics and short stories published in 2012. In 2013, a year after "The Legacy Anthology" was published, Johnson got into a motorcycle accident, but was ok. He was driving 70 miles per hour early morning to Hudson when a deer ran out in front of him. He hit the deer and lost control of his motorcycle. He was wearing a helmet and leather.

Johnson has plans to publish, "Red Dragon Fantasy II: Song Lyrics and Poetry" and is in production of writing four song lyric books.

There were a few attempts to start a band during high school, but it never materialized. In 1999, Johnson met a drummer and guitarist from Baldwin Wisconsin and they did some jamming and had some ideas of the kind of music that they wanted to produce. The drummer, who was kind of the leader, wanted to go into a Red Chili Peppers and Live direction while Johnson wanted to go into a more Metallica and Pantera direction, producing heavy metal, speed metal and thrash.

After the drummer announced that he would be choosing a vocalist that was more purer. Johnson was relieved and decided to stick with only writing song lyrics and continue writing stories as well as illustrating. Johnson never found his soulmate for music since the guitarist he worked with while at Steven's Point Wisconsin aka "Arts World". They worked so well together putting together "Does It Really Matter II" that it was a shame it didn't continue and Johnson didn't want to keep writing love songs or love ballads. He wanted to write and sing in a band that was innovative with raw guitars and drums.

Johnson's ability to write song lyrics continues to grow more intricate and complex. Although he couldn't have gotten there without his father pushing him into it. His biggest influences through his tough times that helped him was Metallica, Pantera, Megadeth, KMFDM,

Guns and Roses and AC/ DC.

A lot of the song writing Johnson does now is from other people's experiences, the news and the internet instead of writing about himself.

www.ingramcontent.com/pod-product-compliance
Lightning Source LLC
Chambersburg PA
CBHW062040220426
43662CB00010B/1582